Othe
Churc

M000312403

**Church Starting and Growth**

**English**

Daniel R. Sánchez, Ebbie C. Smith, and Curtis Watke, *Starting Reproducing Congregations: A Guidebook for Contextual New Church Development.* Ft. Worth, Texas: Church Starting Network, 2001.

Daniel R. Sánchez, Ebbie C. Smith, and Curtis Watke. *Starting Reproducing Congregations Strategy Planner: A Workbook for Contextual New Church Development.* Ft. Worth, Texas: Church Starting Network, 2001.

Ebbie C. Smith, *Growing Healthy Churches: New Directions for Church Growth in the 21st Century.* Ft. Worth, Texas: Church Starting Network, 2003.

Daniel R. Sánchez & Rudolofo González. *Sharing the Good News with Our Roman Catholic Friends.* Ft. Worth, Texas: Church Starting Network, 2004.

Daniel R. Sánchez, *Gospel in the Rosary.* Ft. Worth, Texas: Church Starting Network, 2004

Ebbie C. Smith. *Spiritual Warfare for 21st Century Christians.* Ft. Worth, Texas: Church Starting Network, 2005.

Daniel R. Sánchez, ed. *Church Planting Movements in North America.* Ft. Worth, Texas: Church Starting Network, 2007.

Daniel R. Sánchez, *Hispanic Realities Impacting America: Implications for Evangelism and Missions.* Ft. Worth, Texas: Church Starting Network,

i

Ebbie C. Smith, *Basic Churches are Real Churches*. Ft. Worth, Texas: Church Starting Network, 2009

Ebbie C. Smith, *You, the Missionary: Committing To and Participating in God's Worldwide Mission*. Ft. Worth, Texas: Church Starting Network, 2009.

## Spanish

Daniel R. Sánchez, Ebbie C. Smith, and Curtis Watke, *Como Sembrar Iglesias en el Siglo XXI*.

Daniel R. Sánchez, Ebbie C. Smith, and Curtis Watke, *Mis Planes Estratégicos Para Sembrar Iglesias en El Siglo XXI: Libro de trabajo para el desarrollo contextual de una iglesia nueva*. Ft. Worth, Texas: Church Starting Network, 2002.

Daniel R. Sánchez & Ebbie C. Smith, *Cultivando Iglesias Saludables*. Ft. Worth, Texas: Church Starting Network, 2008.

Daniel R. Sánchez & Rodolfo González. *Comparta Las Buenas Nuevas Con Sus Amigos Católicos*. Ft. Worth, Texas: Church Starting Network, 2004.

Daniel R. Sánchez. *Evangelio En El Rosario*. Ft. Worth, Texas: Church Starting Network, 2004.

Daniel R. Sánchez. *Iglesia: Crecimiento y Cultura*. Ft. Worth, Texas: Church Starting Network, 2004.

Daniel R. Sánchez. *Manual para Implementar Crecimiento y Cultura*. Ft. Worth, Texas: Church Starting Network, 2004.

Daniel R. Sánchez. *Realidades Hispanas Que Impacta A América: Implicaciones para Evangelización y Misiones*. Ft. Worth, Texas: Church Starting Network, 2006.

J.O. Terry, *Guía Para La Narrativa Bíblica* (Synopsis of the Bible Storying Handbook, translated into Spanish by Keith Stamps). Ft. Worth, Texas: Church Starting Network, 2008.

## Bible Storying Resources

J.O Terry, *Basic Bible Storying*. Ft. Worth, Texas: Church Starting Network, 2006.

Daniel R. Sánchez, J.O. Terry, LaNette Thompson. *Bible Storying for Church Planting*. Ft. Worth, Texas: Church Starting Network, 2008.

J.O. Terry, *Bible Storying Handbook: For Short-Term Church Mission Teams and Mission Volunteers*. Ft. Worth, Texas: Church Starting Network, 2008.

J.O. Terry, *Hope Stories from the Bible*. Ft. Worth, Texas: Church Starting Network, 2008.

Daniel R. Sánchez and J.O. Terry. *LifeStory Encounters*. Ft. Worth, Texas: Church Starting Network, 2009.

J. O. Terry, *Death Stories from the Bible*. Ft. Worth, Texas: Church Starting Network, 2009.

J. O. Terry, *Food Stories from the Bible*. Ft. Worth, Texas: Church Starting Network, 2009.

J. O. Terry, *Grief Stories from the Bible*. Ft. Worth, Texas: Church Starting Network, 2009.

J. O. Terry, *Water Stories from the Bible*. Ft. Worth: Church Starting Network, 2009.

*The Church Starting Network supplies all of these resources:*

*www.ChurchStarting.net*

*3515 Sycamore School Road, Fort Worth, Texas 76133*

# Oralizing

# Bible Stories

## For Telling


J. O. Terry

**Oralizing Bible Stories for Telling**

© Copyright 2010 by J. O. Terry

**All rights reserved**

Library of Congress Cataloging-in-Publication Data

J. O. Terry

ISBN 978-0-9846207-0-8

1.      Bible Storying 2. Orality 3. Telling Bible Stories

Cover Picture: Artist Caloy Gabuco, *Peter Preaching in Jerusalem*, "Telling the Story...", International Mission Board, SBC and New Tribes Mission.

vi

# Foreword

In the early days of Bible Storying few resources served as guides for selecting, preparing, and telling Bible stories to those who needed to hear them. Examples from history told of the use of Bible stories and how listeners responded to the stories, but told nothing of how stories were prepared or adapted for telling. Those who rediscovered the value of chronological Bible teaching in the Philippines did provide some basic theological guidelines for selecting the stories to tell and teach. But little material existed to help prepare the stories for sharing with primarily oral learners among my listeners.

This writer soon discovered that Bible stories needed thoughtful preparation related to worldview characteristics of the listeners. Only when this preparation was involved would Bible storyer reach the intended objectives of the best reception, understanding, retention, and retelling by listeners.

Little by little I learned much of what follows as I attempted to prepare and learn the stories and find how best to communicate the Bible stories to those I was training and to those I had the privilege of telling the Bible stories in village gatherings and radio listener rallies.

This is not a book of rules, but of suggested guidelines gained from observation and personal experience. Hopefully the lessons I learned will help the new Bible storyer to become competent and effective early in their Bible Storying experience.

I owe a debt of gratitude to my many interpreters and to my many rural and tribal friends who patiently endured my teaching, even correcting and instructing me along the way. And I owe a special tribute to God who called me to this ministry and placed the burden on my heart for taking the Bible stories of Good News of forgiveness of sin and salvation through faith in Jesus to those waiting to hear.

May God bless the reader as you follow my journey into Oralizing Bible Stories for Telling.

J. O. Terry, Ft. Worth, Texas

# Contents

ix

# Chapter 1

## About the Author and
## His Experiences

I have a background in radio program production and broadcasting. Appointed as a media missionary to the Philippines in 1968, I soon realized that much of what was being done in media ministry was not locally reproducible. I clearly perceived this fact one night while out with a Filipino evangelist for a film showing in a province south of Manila. The film that night was *The Parable of the Persistent Widow* that Jesus told regarding prayer. During the film the evangelist turned to me and said: "If I had a film projector and films, a sound system and screen, and a car to carry the equipment, then I could win people to faith in Jesus just like you."

This comment planted the thought that a better way to preach and teach would be to make the method locally reproducible and empower new local leaders to carry on the teaching. Radio programming through the Philippine Baptist Mission of the International Mission Board was highly successful at the time. It incorporated a series of traditional preaching/worship programs, Bible teaching programs, meditation programs, youth music programs with interviews and counseling, and several drama programs based on real-life events. Mail response for spiritual counsel and enrolment in the Bible Correspondence Course poured in. The Bible Course brought listeners to faith in Christ and began the discipling. Additional lessons provided information on how the listener as a new believer could in turn use the Bible Correspondence course lessons to teach others.

Leaders in rural areas were developing two theological training tracks. One track was a very basic Lay Evangelism and Discipling course (LEAD) led by commuting teachers and through audiocassette lessons. The other was a more literate programmed instruction

1

Theological Education by Extension (TEE) developed to be a self-study programmed instruction course. Low literacy, low education, and low incentive to maintain self-study discipline partially defeated the TEE program causing it to require commuting teachers as well for the oral learners.

A desire for the mission to enter into tribal work led to frustrations due to lack of experience in working with rural peoples who were often nonliterate. Various aspects of limited educational opportunities prevented many tribals from learning to read. Other rural people were functionally nonliterate due to limited education and lack of reading materials, and the oral communication preference common for those living in an oral society.

New Tribes missionaries since 1975 had been contemplating a chronological Bible teaching method that was being used by an Australian missionary on the island of Palawan. This missionary shared his thinking with others of his mission who were attracted to the chronological Bible teaching concept. All the New Tribes missionaries at that time were conducting Bible translation work, teaching literacy, and evangelizing those they worked among.

Due to the Australian missionary's influence, and based on his teaching model, several sets of chronological Bible teaching lessons emerged. These teaching lessons were for the most part expositional teaching of basic doctrinal concepts following a chronological path through the Old Testament and Gospels. Several other New Tribes missionaries felt that their tribal peoples learned best through stories and adapted the chronological Bible lessons into paraphrased Bible story lessons. The lessons, as they came to be shared, were back translated from Philippine languages into English for a wider distribution.

During the early 1980's, New Tribes missionaries shared this new chronological Bible teaching methodology through conferences with missionaries of the Philippine

Baptist Mission. Copies of several Bible story lesson sets were translated into English, printed, and made available. Some missionaries of the Philippine Baptist Mission began teaching the chronological Bible story lessons as these were initially in the same Filipino language they used in their own ministries.

Several years later, after a companion set of Bible teaching pictures was jointly developed by New Tribes Mission and Philippine Baptist Mission, one of the field administrators thought it good to share these pictures and accompanying Bible story lesson sets with workers in other countries. Twenty-five sets of the *God and Man*[1] Bible story lesson books and *"Telling the Story..."*[2] chronological Bible teaching pictures were shipped to Bangladesh where the predominant religion was Islam with a minority being of either Hindu or tribal animistic backgrounds. Since I was the media resource person, the local mission asked me to teach how to use these new resources effectively.

By this time several of the missions in neighboring countries were attempting to operate audiocassette-based training programs for rural leaders. These efforts met with mixed success in that some projects worked well with effective lessons and others either proved "too literately organized" or "too deep" for rural listeners. Lessons were programmed for use on hand-cranked audiocassette players so the programming had to be broken up into five-minute modules that are a typical amount of time a person could crank without lagging. Various other forms of powering the players was tried using local batteries that not only had a short life in use, but also proved too tempting for use in other devices. Some leaders tried solar-panel rechargers and lead acid gel cells but these proved costly, prone to failure when mishandled, and also were often used for powering other devices. In short, there were many issues regarding audiocassette player maintenance and operation in places without electricity. So a better way of disseminating the Bible teaching

3

leading to salvation, discipling, and church planting was definitely needed. At this time affordability and reproducibility were the primary considerations and not yet orality related to low literacy and oral preference for learning.

Meanwhile I had written a paper proposing a move to "People-Powered Media."[3] This approach called for all the teaching to be done *live* by persons who had been trained by another person. Each "teacher" was to be taught by the same methodology the trainees would use in teaching others. Without a really good understanding of the dynamics of deep rural and tribal situations, I was laying initial groundwork for oral-based teaching and training that was people-powered in the region where I worked. Chris Ammons then working among tribals in Peru affirmed this in his paper "Third Generation Thinking"[4] in which he asks the questions:

> Will the learner be able to teach this as effectively as I do?" and "Am I doing anything that will prevent my student's learners from being able to pass on the message just as effectively as I am passing it on?

Literature emerged to help train teachers in this method of story-telling and how to train local leaders to use the method. One part of this literature is the textbook *Basic Bible Storying.*[5] This book, *Oralizing Bible Stories for Telling*, is an expansion of the chapter on "Crafting Bible Stories for Telling" in that text.

# Chapter 2

# Initial Failure Pointed
# To Needed Changes

When the exported chronological Bible lessons from the Philippines failed to produce the same kind of response in other countries as had been experienced in the Philippines, I began investigating what made the Bible teaching materials work in one place and not another. I discovered that some of the people responded well to the paraphrased story content but had difficulty with the expositional teaching format. Later I discovered the dynamic that simply telling the Bible stories produced a good response among all listeners in the villages. Listeners related to the told stories and wanted to talk about them.

I noted also that some Bible stories did not work as well as others. In short, Bible stories worked better when there was relationship to significant worldview and cultural issues, and when the stories were told as *intact* stories without interrupting the stories to insert comments or teaching. Even in the stories that were well received there was often confusion, omissions, and corruption of details in listener attempts to retell the stories. These observations indicated that some stories were filled with details that could not be handled well by listeners with the result that when listeners attempted to retell the stories they dropped, altered, or confused these facts.

Since most of the listeners could not read, they had to rely solely on what they heard and remembered. If they heard wrongly and did not understand, then they remembered wrongly, and were likely to pass the error along to others. Further, most of the teaching I was doing had to be through interpreters who themselves needed to correctly understand the stories. In the early days I spent much time previewing and correcting the interpreters so they understood the Bible stories from English.

So the idea of editing or preparing the stories for oral telling began to take shape. In some of these cultures holy books like the Bible, if translated, were in a high or literary language unlike the vernacular the average person spoke in daily conversation. The words were nice to hear when read aloud because of the poetry and formal expressions of the language, but not always easy to understand. Some listeners had translated Bibles in their spoken language but could not read them with understanding. Other listeners spoke or had limited literacy in the regional or country language, but really needed to hear the stories in their heart language to understand the stories.

Because I did not speak all the languages where I was telling the Bible stories in villages and teaching the stories to leaders, I had to use interpreters. Some of these interpreters had worked with missionaries in traditional teaching of evangelism and discipling lessons and preaching, but not in telling Bible stories as I was doing. In the beginning it was slow going as I was teaching partly from memory and partly from the Bible pages. After going through the same Bible stories several times I was learning to teach more from memory. Further, my interpreters were learning the Bible stories and becoming smoother in how they continued the stories without grasping for a way to express the words and actions of characters, or lapsing into preaching, or just summarizing the words I was saying.

In a few cases Bible stories, as I told them, had to go through double translation from English to a regional language, and then from the regional language into a mother tongue. Consequently, the English Bible story had to be durable—simple enough to remain coherent and intelligible through this process. I recall a time in Bhutan when I was teaching Bible stories to a mixed group of Nepalis and Bhutanese. I was speaking in English. The first interpreter then repeated my words in Nepali. The second interpreter then took the words either from the

English or the Nepali and repeated them in *Dzongka*. I distinctly remember nearly forgetting where I was in the stories when the second interpreter was finished several minutes later! The multiple translation process produced clearer reception of the stories on the one hand but eventuated in some confusion on the other. Several times I recall one of the interpreters saying, "You can't say that!" And we had to back up and try again.

In more than one instance I had interpreters grow confused and ask me to repeat what I said more simply so they would understand it well enough to interpret it properly. In addition, I had some amusing times when I attempted to help my interpreters by using the listeners' own language, only to have my interpreter put it back into English! We usually enjoyed a good laugh on these occasions.

Speaking of interpreters, I had several categories of them. Of course, the very best situation is to have one who is very proficient in English and capable of clear communication in their national language, and who interprets just what you say without adding to it or leaving anything out. My interpreters did have permission to explain simple things that were confusing or unusual to listeners. Usually they would ask me to pause the story while they did so. Outside of the occasional times when an interpreter did not know a certain word or how to express a key Bible term, the interpretation went well as we worked cooperatively in tandem, improving with each session. Questions that listeners asked following a story were often a clue to difficulties in understanding a story. So knowing this helped to revise future story wording for greater clarity.

Some interpreters, however, were like an older one I had who was a former high-caste Hindu. He was well grounded theologically, but in another sense knew too much. Because of his extensive knowledge of the Bible, he constantly expanded what I was telling and added details beyond what I was providing. In addition, at times he would turn to me and say, "I've already told about that!" This explanation, of course, left me wondering what he had told the listeners. Since I was metering out the prepared story in a certain way, the announcement would leave me wondering what to do next. His expanded story usually became evident when the listeners were retelling the stories during practice times. The interpreter's extraneous comments sometimes did not make sense, but the listeners faithfully repeated them anyway in their retelling of the stories.

A young man who was a convert from Islam illustrates another type of interpreter. He constantly summarized what I was saying and usually truncated (left out) key things I had included in the story as I told it. I would mention story characters like Abraham and Sarah but then would not hear these names when he repeated my words in Bengali. I would repeat my words again, emphasizing the names, but again I would hear only a summary of what I said but no names. So I would need to say something like: "This is about Abraham and Sarah." And finally I would hear the names in Bengali.

On one occasion I told the story of *The Gadarene Demoniac* and came to the part about the evil spirits entering the herd of pigs and causing them to rush headlong into the sea. My interpreter became overjoyed with the thought of the pigs perishing and sounded gleeful to the point of causing the listeners to begin laughing. Later, I found out that he had the pigs in his version rushing backwards down the hillside into the water. Why backwards, I'll never know. From his Islamic background I assume that he was simply overjoyed at the death of the unclean pigs.

As the Bible Storying methodology began to develop and storying sessions took shape, retelling the story by listeners became an important participation activity. The initial reason for this was to let the listeners hear the story again in their own language by one of their own people, and secondly, to give the listeners an opportunity to participate in the teaching by retelling the Bible stories.

An even greater benefit for the missionary storyer came from these story retellings. It provided feedback about how the stories were being heard by listeners and what listeners were keeping in their retelling, what the listeners omitted, and what listeners confused or corrupted, usually related to their culture. This feedback then was useful in preparing durable stories so that changes by listeners were minimized, heading off any processing or restructuring of the stories by listeners as they in turn shared the stories with others. This area of possible problem became the focus of the tension between verbatim accuracy of Bible wording on the one hand and on the other hand oral comprehension and faithful retelling of stories by listeners. My object as a storyer was to keep the stories as accurate as possible while shaping the stories for easy comprehension, practical accuracy and retention in memory by the listeners. And to minimize changes the listeners might make in their retelling the Bible stories.

A prevailing belief contends that oral communicators have fantastic hearing and memories for repeating verbatim what they hear. As it turned out, most of the listeners in the countries where I worked tended to hear selectively and especially picked up on things close to their culture or relational to their gender or way of life. Many of the details in the original stories were simply lost in the retelling, usually because the listeners did not understand the relevance of the details to the stories. Conversely some details were of great importance to listeners, though often minimized or even omitted by storyers like myself, either in effort to simplify the stories, or in ignorance of local worldview and interest.

I soon learned that excessive character names in the stories beyond those directly involved in the main storyline could be confusing to listeners. Additionally, details like numbers, especially large numbers, were confusing and often dropped in retelling.

Once I was chastised by a literate Marwari tribal man in Pakistan who was upset because I left out the account of the sending out the birds in *The Flood Story*. I told the story simply in an attempt to reduce the number of details in a long story. The listener in effect told me that I did not understand the story. Then he added that birds as omens were very significant among his people and thus important to the story. However, some of the numbers like the dimensions of the Ark were omitted. The time period of the flood was described as "many days" rather than a verbatim numerical amount.

Other matters that early storyers considered involved decisions about how many proper names could be retained in a story without causing confusion for listeners related to the storyline. What should be done about abstractions like large numbers that were difficult for listeners to process (more on this later)? Some of the structure of character dialog dealt with how story character dialog quotes were handled, whether all of the character dialog was retained or not, and making clear who was speaking to whom using proper names and nouns rather than pronouns. Dialog complicates stories as will be explored later. But character dialog adds greatly to story interest for oral communicators. I discovered this fact after preparing 90 Bible story lessons (*God and Woman*) for Muslim women in which I either summarized the dialog or just simply narrated what was happening in the stories. During field testing women listeners did not like the stories, saying the stories were not interesting. The women wanted the dialog; they wanted to overhear the story characters speaking to one another.

So at the end of the day I witnessed all these things and really saw the answer to the dilemma from the time with the Filipino evangelist and the film. Rather than relying on equipment and imported media programs like films, why not teach the people directly from the Bible in a format they could easily understand, remember, recall and retell? This could be cost effective and easily expanded as outreach continued. And it was something that the local people could do themselves to reach their own people.

Bible Storying as a method had provided an avenue for learning much about oral learners and teaching Bible lessons to oral learners so they could in turn accurately teach others without having to go through a literacy process. No expensive equipment was required. Support budget for training was mainly needed to initiate the teaching while the Bible Storying could continue in the everyday life of the people without the need for outside support. The methodology was culturally appropriate, educationally effective, and best of all, it was readily reproducible by listeners. Needed was packaging the Bible stories for the oral learners by taking the good literate Bible passages and oralizing them to facilitate telling and understanding.

In addition to a number of texts and booklets related to the methodology and practice of Bible Storying, I have also prepared and shared as models a number of Bible story sets based on my experiences and the needs I encountered. These Bible story sets reflect both the concepts described in this book and also reflect the progress of change and learning from those story models developed early in my Bible Storying ministry. There is noticeable difference between my later and my earlier story sets I employed before I had experienced significant time working among oral learners and making first attempts to craft or oralize Bible stories for listeners' understanding.

At present as I write this I am working with some who are preparing Bible stories for Native Americans. I discovered that for many of these peoples names are not used. Instead the story characters go by descriptive names. God becomes "Creator." Adam becomes "first man" and Eve "first woman." The original Hebrew names were descriptive and later formalized into names. And some believe that stories are too holy to be discussed after telling the story. So how to handle learning and teaching from stories without a post-story dialog? So this is an ongoing learning process for Bible storyers as we encounter each new listener group, their literacy competency and their culture.

In Asia I had many listeners, especially among women, asking about the meaning of names in the stories. In one of the story sets for women (*Grief Stories from the Bible*) I included an appendix that listed Bible names in the stories and their meaning. LaNette Thompson in Africa told of a Jula woman asking to hear the story again about the woman who had the same name as hers. Her name was "Hawa;" we know the woman as "Eve."[6]

# Chapter 3

## The Need for Oralizing
## Bible Stories

The following thoughts regarding Bible Story crafting come from the experiences mentioned in the previous chapter. What I share in this book, however, should not be taken as prescriptive or absolute. I share these concepts primarily as descriptive of the teaching and learning tensions that result from taking the Bible as stories to a people who learn best by story and most likely will teach others just as they have learned—through retelling the stories. As a communicator, I want listeners to understand, and as a trainer I want listeners to be able to accurately reproduce understandable teaching that their own people need to hear. Obviously, if the teaching comes from the lips of one of their own people, it reduces the foreignness of the teaching.

Initially I did not use any term for describing Bible story preparation for telling. In some early instances I used the term "editing Bible stories for telling" but this often brought distress to those who thought that the Bible was being tampered with or somehow changed to fit an agenda. So later the term, "story crafting," came into use and has been widely used by myself and others since the early 1990s. The concept of Bible Storying is still occasionally misunderstood by those new to Bible Storying and by those who do not understand the dynamic of teaching oral learners and therefore question or criticize the process of preparing Bible stories for telling and comprehension by listeners.

In addition, description of the process of adapting Bible stories for telling has led to a division into those who do adapt and those who don't, preferring verbatim stories. Among those who adapt Bible stories for telling some prefer staying close to original organization and wording though making helpful or needed adaptation. Others who adapt Bible stories tend to use some degree of paraphrasing to further shape the stories to emphasize certain truths within the stories. This is not necessarily bad for those who can read the stories but not good for those who must rely upon primarily only what they hear.

Other prospective biblical storytellers are reticent to alter the written Word into an oral vernacular. Field experience where firsthand feedback is obtained from listeners will help to encourage a more flexible view on this process. Coming out of literacy experience in Malawi, workers suggested that an oral Bible story used in the literacy program not be written down until it was told several times and perhaps went through a couple generations of retelling to see what oral form it settled into.[7]

I encourage the reader to change the term to whatever expression he/she is comfortable using. Tom Steffen, former New Tribes missionary and chronological Bible teacher in the Philippines (now teaching Intercultural studies at Biola University) has used the term "story smithing" in his text.[8] Paul Koehler uses the term "story scripting" to describe the process he favors.[9]

When I was introduced to chronological Bible teaching in late 1987, I was also introduced to the concept of taking the existing popular paraphrased Bible story lessons in the Philippines and teaching them *as is*. When these stories in written form did not work well as shared with me, I went back to the original Bible wording of the stories and redeveloped the stories until I found a format that seemed to be easily understood by my interpreters and listeners, and that the listeners could remember and reproduce reasonably well. In the beginning this process was largely trial and error. I prepared the stories and told them. Listeners were then asked to retell the stories they had learned. Feedback from this retelling provided clues to what might need shaping for a more accurate retelling of the stories. Sometimes my first knowledge of a problem came from the reaction of other listeners who understood the language. Sometimes they corrected the storyteller and sometimes the others just laughed at the changes. I had to encourage my interpreters to be honest with me and not attempt to fix the story as they relayed it back to me. In this way I learned what was working and what was not, or was likely to be changed or corrupted.

In the beginning I didn't call the story crafting process by any descriptive terminology. As I was teaching and sharing with other missionaries, however, I found that I needed to call the crafting process something. I settled on the term "crafting" as the process involved not only adapting already coherent stories (stories intact as a passage at one reference) but also other stories and groups of stories that needed to be told at the same time. I also compiled needed stories from scattered scripture references into coherent narratives. So I came to use "crafting" and many storyers picked up the term from my shared training materials. The debate, however, lingers on about the audacity of editing God's Word by crafting or any other process.

In time, as the focus on Orality intensified, I begin to consider changing the name of story preparation to "oralizing" Bible stories for telling. This, of course, means taking verbatim written stories that have been prepared for literate readers with good grammar and interesting sentence construction, and adapting the stories into good oral format stories for telling, comprehension, and remembering by oral learners. Other considerations included simplifying or altering stories as needed so that interpreters could easily and accurately grasp the story as I told it, and the listeners could easily follow the story, understanding it without confusion.

This method still provided for the possibility of needed paraphrasing some stories used for bridging (connecting) between major stories when a detailed story would break the continuity between the key stories, and compiling some needed stories from scattered scripture references. Examples of compiled stories are *The Creation of the Spirit World*, or the summary story of *The Prophet's Message of the Messiah* (See these illustrated in a later chapter).

I leave the decision on what to call the process up to the reader or new Bible storyer. When I use the term "Oralizing Bible stories for telling" you will know that I mean doing whatever is needed to make the stories easily understandable, memorable, and reproducible for oral learners as listeners, while always keeping the accuracy of the verbatim story in view. And just for the record, I still favor the verbatim Bible story if it can be used effectively without confusion and distortion, and will not be unreasonably altered by listeners as they attempt to remember it and reproduce it. Fortunately, most of the Gospel stories of the miracles and parables of Jesus are good to go "as is" without needing any drastic crafting outside of some attention mainly to how the character dialog is handled. And many of the Old Testament stories are also good as written, except for some of the longer ones and those with numbers and geographical place names that are not essential to understanding the story and what it teaches.

Readers might want to notice how Stephen oralized Old Testament stories (Acts 7:1-53) in his reply to the religious leaders. The object remains the same—to preserve the accuracy of the original written story as well as to form the story so that it is not only "oral" but also memorable and hopefully, reproducible by listeners.

The bottom line in what I have learned is to be able to tell the Bible stories so they are clearly heard and understood, and to anticipate making the needed adaptations to each story (always staying as close as possible to the verbatim) so that oral learners will receive a told story that is as close as possible to the way they will likely remember it and retell it. In other words, the stories, once oral and now literate, written in a book as good literature, must now be adapted as good oral accounts for telling, hearing, remembering, and retelling.

Interestingly, I never intended to write down my early Bible story sets as they were developed as oral models and taught as oral models. Later when missionaries asked for copies of the stories I was using, some of these story sets were written out as I recalled them from memory. As oral models the stories and lessons were never told or taught exactly the same way each time used. So I worked from memory and responded differently to each teaching situation. Those being trained took home with them an oral story set from which to work.

Many of my interpreters did like to keep an open Bible before them for reference as they interpreted for me. The principles of crafting or oralizing the stories still apply whether preparing oral or written sets of stories. At the end of a curriculum development diagram for Bible Storying, I point out that the stories can be shared in one of three formats: as an *oral set* (not written), be listed in a *template or shell outline* that gives the source scriptures, story title, and any helpful worldview information or discussion questions but no story, or as a complete *written set* of stories that reflect the suggested adapted wording for clear and understandable sharing among oral learners and any learning/teaching activities.

It is, therefore, the purpose of this book to share the things learned in my actual experience preparing, telling, and teaching the Bible stories so that the new Bible storyer will be able to get a head start and hopefully not have to make the same mistakes as this Bible storyer made. Also, I supply these thoughts so that new storyers will not have to take the same length of time to become competent oral communicators.

17

When people balk at "crafting" (the term and/or concept), I like to ask them why we have four Gospels in our Bible. God has already demonstrated that there's more than one acceptable way to tell His story. He has inspired tellers to shape His story for different audiences and different objectives. The Bible itself shows the possibility of varying the presentation in keeping with objective and audience while also being faithful to the essential message.

Admittedly the writers of the Bible were inspired and we are not, but in principle the Bible itself is testimony that God's purposes can be achieved with varied accounts of the same basic events. In fact, God sometimes has more variation among the four Gospels than we are comfortable with! Grant Lovejoy, in relation to this question said, "I wonder if those who are squeamish about 'editing' the Bible tell in full the stories where there are details that make us uncomfortable or where the discrepancies seem pretty striking."[10]

Let me end this chapter with some typical questions that come my way related to adapting or crafting Bible stories for telling:

Q: *Why don't you teach the listeners to read and give them a Bible of their own instead of going through all this process of telling the stories?*

A: It would take a whole chapter to cover all the reasons why the Bible stories need to be told. Literacy is very slow in coming among many people who have little to read and have learned to get along very well without literacy. To stop the process of teaching the stories to instead work on bringing all peoples to literacy would deprive many of ever hearing the Gospel in their lifetime. And we have seen that what we tell and teach orally does spread among a people as they pass it on.

18

Q: *What is all the fuss over changing Bible stories before you tell them?*

A: The Bible translators have done well in preparing good literature and preserving the accuracy of the text. To share this good literature orally so that listeners can hear and understand it, stories also need to be good oral accounts—that is put into an oral form that the listeners are accustomed to hearing and understanding. In addition, this may mean reducing the load of names and some other details that are difficult for listeners to make sense of when hearing the story, but that essentially do not change the storyline or intent of the story when left out.

Q: *Aren't you uncomfortable with "making up" stories and saying they are in the Bible?*

A: Some of the stories that we have discovered needing in actual practice are not "made up" but are rather compiled into coherent narratives from pieces that are found in different scripture references throughout the Bible. One such story is *The Creation of the Spirit World* that uses many Bible references told as a coherent story that helps explain that God did not create evil spirits, but some spirits rebelled and became evil spirits, and that God as Creator is sovereign over even the unseen spirit world. Assembling *The Prophets' Story of the Messiah* into a narrative is a helpful summary that introduces and transitions into the Gospel stories of Jesus.

Q: *If some stories are so difficult to tell and understand by listeners, why not just tell the easy ones?*

A: To do so, I would be denying listeners some of the better stories that may speak more clearly to their hearts and also in effect denying listeners some of the counsel of God. In addition, some of the longer stories may in fact be more relational for listeners and much appreciated.

Q: *If you leave details out of long stories, won't listeners miss out part of the story and misunderstand the story?*

A: In actual practice we find that shortening long stories often helps not only the understanding of the story but the possibility that listeners will remember it more accurately without gaps and confusion, and be able to retell it fluently.

Q: *If all Scripture is inspired and profitable, isn't removing or changing part of it unscriptural?*

A: Yes, we must be careful with what we alter in any way or leave out. Yet there are many details in some stories that do hinder oral learners and those not familiar with all the geographical details of the Holy Land. In addition, concepts like large numbers often don't really convey meaning to oral listeners. I have been with people that a quantity like "three thousand" would just be words without any meaning. But if I said "like trees in a forest" or "stars in the sky," this would suggest great quantity.

Q: *Why don't you use the people's Bible and just tell or read the stories to the listeners?*

A: Some people have Bibles only in a regional language and not in their conversational language. These may be generally understandable, but often have unfamiliar or uncommon words that are difficult to understand clearly. In addition, some cultures have Bibles that as holy books are written in a literary language that is nice to hear but not easy for the average person to understand. One of my favorite interpreters was a college graduate in journalism and was highly literate. He remarked that after he heard me tell the stories, then he could read them and understand them in his Bengali Bible that was an archaic high literary language translation dating back to the early 1800's in the time of William Carey. A newer translation has since come out that is more readable. Many rural peoples have a simpler conversational language with a more limited vocabulary as well as their own idiomatic expressions.

Let me end the questions here. It is good that those new to Bible Storying are asking all these questions. All that many of us do by selecting Bible stories to tell and preparing them for our oral learner listeners has been to overcome difficulties in communicating God's Word clearly to the listeners, and empowering them in turn to share it with others in this present generation. We are seeing many people have access to the Bible who did not have it previously. Many of these people understand the stories leading to their salvation, to the planting of new churches, and to their maturing as believers. In God's time we pray that many more will become literate and have a Bible in their own spoken language and be able to read with understanding. Until that time comes we will continue to share key Bible stories and other passages with the wisdom and experience that God has given us.

Later I will mention the matter of providing an Oral Bible. Perhaps a better description would be to call it Oral Scripture.

As a Bible-Storying trainer, I have remained alert to these and other issues regarding making God's Word orally accessible to those who need to hear it. I rejoice at the progress I've seen in the past two decades at making the Bible accessible using stories, narrated discourse passages, and memory verses for many oral-learner people who never had this privilege previously. We are seeing lives changed and churches planted as a result.

# Chapter 4

## Introduction to
## Story Oralizing

From the beginning of human history people told stories of heroes and myths of their beginnings to recall important past events. These stories probably were not fixed word-for-word in their format, but were recalled in a relaxed manner as the events paraded themselves in the teller's mind. Over time and with repeated retellings stories began to take a more or less fixed form and prescribed vocabulary, or at least fixed phrases that were the building blocks for the stories. This does not mean that later storytellers always followed the stories verbatim as they received them. But many people in that day lived in an oral world that relied on reasonably accurate retelling of stories by recreating the stories as they told them.

Over time among various cultures, persons besides the elders, who were living when things happened, assumed the role of official storytellers, recalling the heritage stories of their people. These leaders retold the stories at auspicious times and repeated the stories often during a person's lifetime. The listeners never tired of hearing the familiar stories, growing fonder with each repetition. It was essential for the storyteller to, at some point in his or her lifetime, have an understudy who listened carefully and learned the stories that they would tell after their mentor was gone. Thus the storytelling tradition was passed down from generation to generation.

Stories were narrated, chanted, sung, danced, or dramatized in their telling. In this way, colorful folk arts developed along with their precious content of a people's history. Before literacy came to a people, this process was always oral, often mixing the verbal and visual in presentation.

Along with the practice of telling the heritage stories, formulae developed using idiomatic expressions and vocabulary that became fixed, along with formats for telling important stories. Some stories were couched in animal tales and totem stories that embodied the essential details, morals, or truths shared by a people. The popular *Jataka Tales* ascribed to the Buddha told of his previous lives as various animals. Others came to be legendary and heroic figures as characters in the stories about their lives and exploits. Certain fixed protocol became commonplace for beginning a story, for stereotyping or describing characters, and for suggesting a moral or reason why the story was being told, and for ending a story. Parabolic and metaphorical stories abounded for those living in concrete relational societies. In time allegorical stories also found their place in support of society and religion.

Some stories that evolved were based on observations and common experiences among a people and in time became condensed into proverbs, which are, in essence, a story cooked down to its bottom line. Some stories, no doubt, were retained more for entertainment value than for instructional purposes. Other stories, definitely having instructive undertones, were provided to warn and admonish about the consequences of wrong behavior or actions, and even to bring hope and to encourage right behavior (See 1 Cor 10:6, 11; Rom 15:4). The psalmist echoed the admonition that God gave to the Israelites through Moses to remember all that had happened (see Deu 6:1-12 and Psa 78:1-7). The consequences of forgetting were noted in Judges 2:10*ff* when the Israelites forgot the stories of God and what He had done for Israel.

Stories have value as an important part of celebration and incorporation into rituals. In the Jewish celebration of the Passover the oldest son asks the father what is the significance of that night which is answered by the father's recalling the story of the Israelites in their suffering as slaves in Egypt when the LORD delivered them after they ate the first Passover. In a similar vein both the Christmas narrative and the Passion narrative have become important parts of our Christmas and Easter celebrations.

The told stories are like both a loaf of freshly baked bread and like comfortable old clothes. Fresh bread has a smell and flavor that stirs up our interest and desire to consume it. As bread becomes stale it loses that fresh-baked initial aroma, texture, and taste, becoming flat and tasteless. New stories are like that freshly baked bread and can be exciting and attractive for a people who may not know where the story is heading because it is unfamiliar. The story may tease and provoke first this response and then another before coming to a resolution, either explicit in the story or implied. Literates generally like the new, the fresh stories that have the smell of adventure that leads into new places and worlds.

Irony adds to the interest with suspense and emotional response to a story if things don't happen as expected, or the character roles are reversed with the stereotyped good characters being the antagonists and the stereotyped bad characters turning out to be the protagonists. In time new stories, more exciting or seen to be more relevant, can displace those formerly new and now fading stories. To survive, the stories are freshened up or revived in new ways of telling. Literate cultures usually have a greater appetite for new and clever stories.

The old clothes characteristic is that of a well-worn story that has been around for some time and is familiar to all, comfortable to hear, loved, and enjoyed each time it is retold. Everyone knows how it will end, but enjoys hearing it again because of the characters and who they portray, the plot and its twists, and the outcome—listeners relive the story each time they hear it. Because everyone knows the stories, and because the stories are repeated often, these stories take on a fixed form and are likely to be preserved in that form from generation to generation. Oral cultures are more comfortable with the familiar, the traditional, and the old stories that listeners already know. But when new stories fill in gaps in knowledge for listeners then these, too, are attractive to oral learners. Stories challenging existing beliefs leading to a cognitive dissonance may cause listeners to outright dismiss a story, to change the story to bring it into agreement with existing beliefs, to hold the story in suspension while continuing to think about it, or to wait in hope of hearing more stories that support or relate to it, or even to allow the new and better stories to displace the old stories.

It has been proven that oral peoples can and often do preserve heritage stories almost verbatim from generation to generation, and place to place. It is also true that storytellers do tinker with the stories, making subtle changes here and there, perhaps enhancing those parts that evoke the greatest response from the listeners.

Storytellers may add comment or explanation to unfamiliar parts when shared among new listeners. So in time stories can drift from their original wording and yet still be basically the same story. This outcome is very common among many of the stories told by Hindu gurus and storytellers where a moral has been encapsulated in a parable. One such example is *The Loincloth—a Parable on Desire*[11] which has several variations, but all centering on the creation of desire which is thought to be the undoing of man in his quest for release from suffering, a common Hindu and Buddhist theme.

Stories that evolve among a people have vocabulary and other story details that are appropriate for that people. One situation faced among Hindus was the need to have a unified and unequivocal reference to God in the stories. It was not enough to say "LORD" or even "God" without giving a more complete name or a name with descriptive such as "Jehovah God" or "Lord Jesus." When I was using the expression "the LORD" in telling the Old

26

Testament stories, one of my interpreters stopped me and corrected me by telling about the need to use a more definite name like "Jehovah God" in storying among Hindus to distinguish the God we know from their pantheon of gods. He reminded me that when I said "the LORD" that a Hindu could add his favorite deity to the name to complete it. So I found it helpful to be consistent in the name used so there was no doubt that only one true God was referred to in the stories. There was also need to be consistent in what name I used for God and not to switch back and forth as happens in a few stories where God and the LORD are used interchangeably. I learned that the several different ways of referring to God or Jesus in Bible stories should be consistent so as not to be confusing.

Among people who do not handle large numbers in their transactions their stories will reflect this in how quantities of things are described. Bible stories which have many numbers like *The Flood Story* may need to be adapted to suggest quantities without using so many numbers. In the NIV account of *The Flood Story* there are thirty numbers or references to numbers. To provide the length of a passage of time could it be like: "After many moons it came to pass..." One person telling an Africanized version of the *Crucifixion Story* gave the time of the crucifixion not as "the third hour" but gestured toward the horizon with his hand and said "When the sun was this high...."

Folk stories generally have few characters and are close-up in how the characters are portrayed—simply and with bold descriptive strokes. This is unlike that of novels in which complex characters are developed layer by layer in several chapters, or in which many characters are introduced before the main plot gets underway.

The problem then comes when new stories are brought in from the outside that do contain details like numbers, extended time frames, inverted stories with flashbacks, multiple intertwined plots, many characters, and geographical settings that are confusing, difficult to understand, socially offensive or even taboo. Role reversals where the good and the bad are reversed according to a Western worldview can be confusing as well. These unfamiliar story elements may make it difficult for listeners to accept, to comprehend fully, to remember, or even to retell such stories accurately. A good story with an important spiritual or moral teaching may thus be lost because of baffling complexity, some culturally inappropriate detail, inappropriate format, confusing character portrayal, or even irony that can offend unless these things are taken into account in preparing the stories for telling.

Oral stories need to be crafted or shaped for effective telling. We all know the consequences of a poorly told joke that founders because it is stated clumsily or the details and punch line are confused or gotten out of order. Even more so is the case with serious stories of life and death. The stories in the Bible, both in the Old Testament and later the Gospels, were originally told orally, in time they were written down in a form that both preserved the stories' original function and meaning and to some extent fixed their structure and content. In use then the stories need to be reconverted back to oral accounts.

Interpreters realize that in translating the Bible into English and other languages things are done to the vocabulary, structure, and grammar of a story to make it good literature for readers. Typical among these are the use of more interesting variety of English grammar constructs like dependent clauses. Pronouns are used in place of repeating proper names and nouns over and over.

Simply translating word for word and telling the stories as presented in the English language formatted Bible can leave oral communicators struggling to keep track of who is saying what to whom. Complicated sentence structure is not good oral sentence structure. Details that are preserved in the written form may overload listeners when dropped on them in the course of telling a verbatim story; even in the listeners' own language. Oral crafting of a written story helps to enhance a story's reception, to make it good "oralture."

This procedure may pose a dilemma for some. In countries where writings that come from a holy book must be in high formal language and not like the vernacular spoken on the street, it may be difficult for a person in that situation to write out a story as it would be spoken, and not in the formal language expected for books. In those countries the use of oral storying models was a way around this dilemma where the stories were learned and told from memory and usually crafted by the teller without ever passing through a written form. This procedure was most difficult to do by seminary trained, literate evangelists and pastors who relied on scripts, but was done naturally by those less literate who functioned as true oral communicators.

This has also been my own personal experience in telling stories and then seeing the same stories retold by oral learner evangelists and pastors. Their retelling reflected cultural influences as well as certain oral prerequisites that shaped the stories for their people. So in working among a people for several years and with many interpreters I had to learn to "pre-shape" a story for better transition from learning the written story in my English language Bible to retelling in local languages, and on to retelling by listeners to their own people in their heart language. This is why I recommend that model story sets in English not be simply translated word-for-word but instead should be redeveloped in the local language of the listeners.

Several concerns are noted: One is that the story as told originally by myself, the Bible storyer, is understood by the first generation listener who in this case was my interpreter. Second, was the need that the second-generation listeners who received the stories from my interpreter accurately understood my interpreter's retelling of the story. My concern continued for the story to travel well for the third generation retelling and beyond. Was it shaped to travel well in subsequent retellings by listeners without losing its original meaning?

Among the special concerns in Bible Storying is to craft stories to encourage attention, interest, and understanding (even enjoyment) of stories. To do this effectively character dialog was needed, though the use of dialog complicated the stories. As mentioned earlier, in the original crafting of Bible stories for the Muslim women's lessons in *God and Woman,*[12] much of the dialog was eliminated to simplify the stories for nonliterate uneducated women. When the stories were presented to the women, however, the stories had lost their lifeblood and along with that the women's interest. For this reason, almost 90 stories had to be "recrafted" to reintroduce character dialog, thus putting life back into the stories.

Entry and background stories that help to explain important things in the main story are also needed for many of the Bible stories. An entry story would be like the exploits of David's mighty men in 2 Samuel 23 in which David's relationship with the father of Bathsheba (Eliam) and husband (Uriah) are introduced as among David's bodyguards who risked their lives to serve and protect David. Similarly a background story would be the resettlement of Samaria by foreigners in 2 Kings 17 in which the spiritual and cultural differences of the Samaritan people are introduced before telling *The Parable of the Good Samaritan* (Luk 10:25ff) or the story of *Jesus and the Samaritan Woman* (Jn 4:4ff). The background story could be crafted and joined to the main story as an introduction or told separately to provide a needed perspective to understand the irony in Jesus' use of the Samaritan as the good neighbor.

Another concern then is to arrive at a story format and content that is durable, more likely to survive and be repeated accurately by the listeners. This can pose a tension. A need exists to know how listeners format and tell their true stories, and whether this is compatible with how Bible stories might be told.

In *Grief Stories from the Bible*[13] I developed the story set based on a practice that Central Asian women have of gathering to share their misfortune stories. In their world the stories are as gross and detailed-filled as possible to garner the maximum emotional response from the listening women. In doing so, the storyteller discharges her own emotion. However, I did not feel a freedom to distort the Bible stories I used in this manner. I included all the detail and emotion that I could find in each story. I slightly refocused some of the stories for the interest of the women and to make them more relative, but essentially kept pretty close to the verbatim story wording and yet ended with how God redeemed each woman's life.

There can be tension in whether to tell a longer story like that of Joseph as a single story with many scenes, details, and characters while preserving the flow of the plot, or to break it up into many smaller component stories with fewer details and characters, and less dialog and plot to remember. Does the interruption of the larger story into component episodes lose the larger storyline? Could the storytellers I was training then reassemble the individual stories and their component episodes into the larger story and its continuing storyline? What about choosing events out of the larger story related to the storying lesson objective, and ignoring others that were interesting but not strategic?

An African elder who heard the entire story of Joseph was asked what "things" he learned from the story. He reflected a moment and then replied with just this one observation: "Joseph never forgot his family!" This is an illustration of the holistic view that many oral communicators have regarding stories that may be loaded with themes, truths, promises and warnings. In this case, therefore, it would be better to craft the longer story with multiple episodes into smaller stories that are bite-size and more representative of one truth or teaching per story. But if the storyer already knows how oral culture listeners might size up a longer story, then the longer story has more weight in emphasizing that one truth or the teaching that listeners are likely to get from the cumulative effect of episodes told as a longer story.

The Passion Story is one story that I have found works better as a single extended story than to break apart and tell individually each of the component episodes. By the time The Passion Story is reached in a typical Bible Storying strategy, considerable foundation is already laid by earlier stories and prophecy for the extended story to make sense as fulfillment. Again and again I've watched the impact of this extended story on listeners as it plunged ahead touching their emotions. But there is also great merit in telling and discussing the individual component stories to focus on the significant truths and themes in them.

The down side is that the longer story will be more difficult to remember and retell by most listeners than individual component stories. This possible disadvantage is, however, offset to some extent by the power of the more complete account.

I experimented with fast-tracking panoramas to give the larger overview with accelerated narrated stories and very limited dialog. Then I went back and told the component stories with the necessary dialog and detail that made the stories more enjoyable for listeners. In the retelling by those being trained I expected and later found to be the case that national storytellers preferred the individual stories which were more entertaining to them and their listeners and not as "dry" as the fast-track panoramas. But the storying trainees consistently stated that the panoramas were very helpful to them in understanding how all the stories fitted together. Probably the most poignant comment came from one young Koch tribal man in Bangladesh who said: "Now I understand why Jesus had to suffer and die."

# Chapter 5

## Stories Can Get Altered

When a Bible story is carried to a new people there may need to be a change in character descriptions, or alterations in how the plot is expressed so that the new listeners will relate to the essential details of the new story. In such cases, contextualization takes place, either deliberately or casually as stories are moved from place to place. Stories that Native American tribes told usually had some adaptability. While the basic accounts of Creation or how the tribe's most revered ceremonies arose would be held sacred and invariant, many other stories could shift as changed circumstances warranted. Following is the account of a story that underwent some adaptation by those who received it from a storyteller outside their tribe.

Frank Cushing, an ethnographer studying Zuni tribes, participated in a round of storytelling. Cushing told a European folk tale of *The Cock and the Mouse*. A year later when Cushing returned and participated in another round of storytelling he discovered that the Zuni had altered the story by adding details to it from their culture. And as a result of their new story ending, the Zunis added their own observation of what happened that explained why cocks have a red comb.[14]

One of the ways that may help to prevent story changes like the preceding is the careful linking of stories with other stories in a matrix or series. This matrix of stories includes any threads that run through the stories to tie them together as part of an ongoing or progressive story. One of the dangers of unlinked stories is that of negative restructuring or reinterpretation by the listeners according to their own experiences. In crafting a series of stories with the same character, look at the larger story first and what ties together the individual episodes so that each of the individual episodes strengthens or supports the others in the series so an individual story cannot be easily reinterpreted or changed because the other stories anchor it.

In another example that I heard regarding a children's story, a mother told her daughter the story of *The Little Red Hen* who had some corn seed and asked the other animals to help her plant the seed. When none did, she planted it herself. When it was time to harvest the corn, the hen asked the other animals to help, but none did. When it was time to grind the corn, she had to do it alone. When she baked the corn into cornbread, no one helped. So when the cornbread was done, the hen took it from the oven and ate it all by herself.

However, when the daughter retold the story, she fixed the story according to her own idea of how it should have ended. She told the early part of the story just as her mother had done until she came to the part about taking the cornbread from the oven. It was then that the little red hen offered some to all the other animals. And all the animals were happy because the little red hen shared her bread.

Jacob Loewen cited an example of an isolated story that lacked a perspective for listeners: A merchant had a companion with a tape recorder and several isolated dramatized accounts of Bible stories with sound effects for the Choco Indians of Panama. The Chocos restructured the garbled message of stories as a continuous whole. Instead of being a message of good news, the stories with their sound effects terrified the Choco listeners to the point they stopped working. As a result the local merchants banded together to rid the community of this terrifying message. [15]

Eugene Nida shared this interesting note: When the Shipibos of Peru heard the story of *The Gadarene Demoniac* and how the evil spirits left the man and entered into the pigs that ran into the lake and drowned, the Shipibos deduced this explained the origin of river dolphins that they called water demons. The whole point of the Bible story was lost as the Shipibos were far more interested in this explanation than in what happened to the demoniac.[16]

What crafting of that story would be needed to preserve the focus on the mastery of Jesus over the evil spirits? Could the story be altered by saying "the pigs died when the evil spirits entered them" in order to avoid the dolphin interpretation? Or should the story be put off until a later time when the listeners would be more interested in Jesus than in the dolphins? A slight change in wording allows us to continue using a powerful story with a strong testimony regarding Jesus without certain story details derailing the main focus and understanding.

Many times I found that some stories in whole or details in stories were considered offensive for various reasons, poorly understood, or were distorted in retelling. Some stories had to be put off for the time being or crafted to carefully avoid or minimize whatever might distract, confuse, or increase hostility that could break relationship. Back translation during practice times in training sessions when participants would retell the stories provided feedback of story details that were troublesome. This opened the door to talk about these issues and as a group to decide what to do.

At times those repeating the stories made significant changes to the stories for various personal reasons. Over time my goal was to minimize this though I knew it could never be completely eliminated. Here are some examples:

I told the story of *Jesus and the Samaritan Woman*. I mentioned that the disciples had left Jesus alone to go into the town to buy food. I saw the puzzled looks on listeners' faces. The listeners were a bit tense throughout the story and I wondered if it was what Jesus was telling the woman. There was something in the story that bothered them. Later as they retold the story in the practice time the trainees were apparently doing something that prevented the puzzled looks I had earlier observed. As the story was retold to me in English I saw what was happening. Those retelling the story had fixed the bad social scene by having one of the disciples to stay back with Jesus for some reason. I learned this was so Jesus was not alone with the woman. For later listeners I altered the story by leaving out the departure of the disciples in order to keep the people listening for the remainder of the story where the important details are.

In stories where a situation is implied that is not socially acceptable to listeners, and thus would raise a flag disrupting listening to the story, it may be wise to consider leaving out the offending detail(s) to keep listeners from stopping listening before hearing the whole story. An alternative is to attempt explaining the situation prior to telling the story, hoping the listeners will accept the matter as permitted for that culture in the story. After the story of the Crucifixion and listeners came to understand who Jesus is, I would go back and retell the whole story with the offending details and then let the listeners talk about that and why it was initially omitted. Also I asked what they would do when telling that story to their own people.

I realize that the Cross is offensive to some religious backgrounds and I would definitely not leave that out of a story. So pray about the matter when faced with a decision to keep or omit and follow the Spirit's leading.

Another instance of changing a story was *The Parable of the Prodigal Son*. Again the listeners changed the story ending to suit their culture. When they retold the story the father consulted with the older son first to see if it were okay for the younger son to return home. In their culture family harmony was very important and the older son would have a significant role in making family decisions. I learned of the change when the story was retold to me in English. My interpreter assured me that was the way the person had changed the story.

The story of Deborah for women presents Deborah and later Jael as brave women. But the story ends with the enemy Sisera entering the tent of Jael whose husband is on friendly terms with the enemy Sisera's king. In the Bible story Jael invites Sisera into her tent and provides him milk to drink. Then she covers him and he falls asleep. While he is sleeping Jael drives a tent peg through Sisera's head and kills him. There are apparently several troubling things in that ending: for a man to enter a woman's tent when her husband is not there, and for the person to be killed while under the protection and hospitality of a tent-dweller. So tellers altered the story for Jael to practice hospitality by offering Sisera milk and then as he lay down under a tree (outside her tent) to cover him and kill him. This apparently fixed the story for those retelling it and kept Jael as a clever and brave woman, but resolved the cultural issues. This proved to be a difficult story to correct because of very deeply ingrained cultural and moral practices.

A missionary in Korea who was teaching Bible stories to seminary students related to me another such incidence of a changed story. In telling the story of *Two Men Who Went to the Temple to Pray* (Luk 18:9-14), one student added to the story a third man who entered the temple to steal the offering and was prevented doing so by the tax collector and so through this good merit the tax collector earned God's acceptance. The storyer had a weak understanding of repentance and a strong belief in earning one's merit (Buddhism), so to him the story needed the third character to make the story happen. The Bible story was lacking this needed story element for him. Similar alterations in stories have occurred in other places. I don't agree in doing this, but it happens. Perhaps if this parable were coupled with the *Story of Zacchaeus* and *The Parable of the Prodigal Son*, then the theme of repentance would be stronger and the parallels in the three stories would focus more on the persons and the change in their lives than on earning merit individually.

With Muslims the Bible stories are more complete and accurate accounts of stories mentioned in the Quran. I've seen attributes of Hindu deities attributed to Jesus and characteristics of typical Indian holy men attributed to the prophets in the Bible stories.

Before examining guidelines for story crafting it is helpful to take a look at some Bible story formats and the relative advantages and disadvantages of each.

# Chapter 6

## Format Options
## For Oralizing Stories

Stories are meant to be told. So stories must be *crafted* for telling. Immediately the storyer is faced with a number of decisions regarding the format of the Bible stories as they will be used in a Bible Storying strategy or ministry opportunity.

Major issues in crafting stories have to do with telescoping very long stories into a manageable size or breaking them up into several component-linked stories or episodes each with their own themes. This procedure allows simplifying long stories that might be confusing, the inclusion of many things new or unfamiliar to listeners or difficult to understand, and dealing with character dialog, narrative comment and any other needed explanations. The outcome must be a story that is:

- "tellable"— that tells well,
- true to the Bible message,
- interesting to listeners,
- and is memorable so that it can be recalled and retold by the listeners.

So the story must "listen well" also. In doing all this we want to avoid "dumbing down" the stories as for those of limited mental capacity, or of deconstructing the stories in any way so they lose their "storyness." The end result is to put the Bible story into an accurate recreated version of the teller's own words. And a Bible story does not need to be long in order to be a good story. Many of the favorite stories are relatively short, but are highly relational for listeners.

The Bible story is the repository of biblical truth that addresses spiritual need, through which God speaks to the listeners. A story that is remembered can continue to speak its message long after the story is first heard. By sharing the told story as a *story*, the truths or elements that are to be communicated are *bound* into the story container and *handed over* to the listeners. If the story is crafted well, it helps the listeners to *unpack* it in dialog or application while still retaining its integrity as a story so that it can be remembered and accurately passed along to others.

One of the disadvantages of expository teaching from a Bible story without telling the story is that the story is unpacked in pieces and handed over to oral-communicator listeners in a literately organized form. They may have no *container* to carry the pieces away and may lack the understanding to reassemble the story accurately. Though the unpacking (teaching) may be very thorough, the listeners are more than likely to carry away familiar pieces that are relational in some way and to leave behind story pieces that don't have a peg in their hearts to hang on. The intact story gives a container for those pieces that can be re-examined at leisure by listeners long after the teaching session. And the story *container* is definitely easier to pass along to others.

Ralph Neighbor once commented during a city evangelism conference in Manila that listeners bring mental baskets of varying capacities and construction to a meeting. Listeners with large baskets can receive and retain much information, especially when contained in a story format. Those with smaller baskets will probably do better with shorter less complex stories that fill their mental baskets. But there may be some listeners that have baskets with holes (due to barriers, lack of experience or perceived relationship) through which teaching fragments may drop out. It is these listeners who benefit most from teaching contained in stories that are not deconstructed into fragments. In other words the intact story provides the needed binding to keep all the fragments as truths and themes bound together.

Since large parts of the Bible were originally handed down orally and memorized to be recited, much of the stories' original oral formatting survives even in written format. Perhaps the best example of this is the Gospel of Mark and its stories that have an oral quality about them — the accounts of each event and discourse are brief and move quickly from event to event. It may well have been a story sermon of Peter that John Mark later recorded for non-Jews. Compare the Gospel of Mark with that of Matthew and its discourses to see the difference. The Gospel of Luke we know to have been a written account as a letter. John mentions at the end of his Gospel that he had intentionally written down the selected accounts of events in Jesus' life so that the readers may believe that Jesus is the Christ, the Son of God, and by believing have eternal life.

Other stories in Genesis, Exodus, Numbers, Joshua, and Judges as well as the books of Samuel, Kings, Chronicles, Ruth, Esther, Jonah, Hosea, and to a less extent Job are "tellable" stories pretty much as they are recorded. In *The Creation Story* and *The Fall* in Genesis there is an economy of words as the story moves along where a mix of dialog, comment, and narrative carry the unfolding plot.

Dr. Grant Lovejoy illustrates the inspired crafting of the Bible stories by examining the story of Jacob and Esau when Jacob bargained for the birthright of Esau (Gen 25:27-34). The Bible narrator skillfully combines descriptive narrative to begin the story, character dialog between Jacob and Esau, and closing comment to tell the story. The narrator's use of verbs (ate, drank, got up, and left) speeds the story along to conclusion after developing the tension between the two brothers and letting the brothers each express their characteristics through their dialog.

There are some other issues that may be important to consider in crafting stories for telling. One is the role of *rhythm* in stories that comes from repeated words and phrases and plot structure that lend a kind of pattern or rhythm to a story. In the story of *The Flood* it is stated three times that Noah did *all* that God commanded him (Gen 6:22, 7:5, 9). In the story of Shadrach, Meshach, and Abednego (Dan 3) the musical instruments are listed four times in the story and provide a kind of rhythm in their listing. This rhythm can be generated in story clustering. For example: in the Gospel of Mark, the author notes three times that Jesus told his disciples what was going to happen to him in Jerusalem, but they did not understand (Mk 8:31ff; 9:31ff; 10:32ff). Again in the prayer in Gethsemane there is a rhythm established in the three times Jesus prayed and returned to find the disciples sleeping.

The last item is that many oral peoples tend to view stories *holistically* in terms of themes or morals they draw from the stories. The listeners may be distracted by unfamiliar or objectionable things in a story because they are not able to distance themselves to see the larger picture from the story because of details that are distracting. Interestingly, this is also true of their visual literacy in examining pictures that may have distracting details. This factor will be mentioned again in examples like that previously mentioned of Jesus being alone with the Samaritan woman which in many South Asian cultures is a socially unacceptable situation, thus interrupting the story for listeners. Mention of Sarah being Abraham's sister as well as his wife is distracting for those who do not marry close clan relatives but perfectly acceptable by others who marry kin to keep property in the family.

Following is a synopsis of story formats that might be used in a storying strategy, either as the primary source story to teach from, or as illustrating/complementary stories like a drama that would follow the told story. I have selected and used certain arbitrary terminology to describe each format. The classifications used are only for sake of having some common basis for categorizing and labeling formats to be able to share the concepts in workshops and training materials among other storyers.

Outside of the verbatim format category there can be considerable overlap of characteristics between format categories as these are not mutually exclusive. The formats differ mainly in degree of change in the story that is permitted to accommodate any of several objectives of accuracy, ease of telling, clarity, sharper focus upon story themes being developed for the storying lessons, time limitations where some bridging of skipped stories is needed, and in some cases to make the stories easier to remember and retell. After a brief description of each format a summary of advantages and disadvantages is given.

This categorization of crafting formats does not necessarily imply that any certain formats are bad or should not be used at all. The storyer should be aware of what is gained and what is lost by the choice of each story format. Choice of format should be compatible with the overall storying strategy and objectives. Following is a listing and description of story formats commonly used in Bible Storying:

**VERBATIM—READING FROM TEXT or RECITING TEXT FROM MEMORY—**No story crafting is involved in this format, as the story is simply lifted out "as is" and "word-for-word." If the story were read from the text, it would be read, as it would be told, that is, with emphasis and pauses to give expression that fosters interest in the story and understanding of story's plot and implication for listeners.

*Advantages:* This method focuses on accuracy and is more acceptable to many Muslims who would be less likely to complain that the storyteller had altered the story. No real story crafting is required, only the need to define beginning and ending of the story. This is the most conservative format for an oral Bible and requires the least amount of preparation for reading or an appropriate memorizing for reciting. One storyer in West Africa said that in her early Bible Storying situations the women listened better when the stories were read.[17]

*Disadvantages:* The storyteller cannot leave out minor characters and excessive details that load the story or items that compete for attention by distracting from the major storyline. It is difficult to handle longer stories that contain multiple themes and many proper names of people and places that load the story with details that may not be essential to understanding the implication of the story for listeners. The reading method requires a literate reader, or one who can memorize verbatim after hearing a story read to them. Verbatim reciting from memory is difficult for literates while some oral communicators can recite even longer stories without extensive study and practice.

This format is a problem when there is no official translation of the Scripture in listeners' heart language. Use of trade or market language reading may be less effective as religious vocabulary may not be understood by all listeners or may reflect borrowing words from the predominant religion. Reading the story requires a literate skill and so is difficult for oral communicators who aren't literate.

***EDITED VERBATIM—READING FROM TEXT or RECITING FROM MEMORY***—This format is a compromise that still retains most original text wording as the unedited verbatim but allows for some minimal selective editing of content to simplify or shorten stories, to improve comprehension, especially by revising character dialog to reflect clearly who is speaking to whom. Generally only deletions of words or phrases are allowed but vocabulary changes are not allowed.

*Advantages:* Same as verbatim but involves selective compression and editing to shorten longer stories and eliminate some distracting storyline elements by ending stories at a suitable closure point without introducing a new issue (*The Flood Story* ending at the rainbow, leaving off the prohibition of eating meat with blood still in it in cultures where this cultural practice needs consideration and understanding, etc.). In some circumstances it may be possible to leave out part of a story that may just be confusing or distracting. If comment asides are needed, these are better done outside the story before beginning the story, or after telling the story if needed to clarify some item or issue related to the actors, location or plot, and any necessary transitions for linking stories. This can permit skipping over intervening stories inserted in the course of a longer story (*Judah and Tamar*, Gen 38 in the story of Joseph).

Edited verbatim also allows conjoining of relevant events (still verbatim) found in another passage (for example: *The Visit of Wise Men* and *Escape to Egypt*, Mat 2) added to Luke's *The Birth of Jesus* story (also see Composite Enhanced Stories). Oral communicators will usually accept this as the way the story is told. Minor crafting is permitted but verbatim wording is kept as much as possible.

*Disadvantages:* Disadvantages are generally few, and are similar to verbatim reading, except by conservative Muslims and semi-literates who may catch minor deletions and changes in the stories. There is possibility of problems when the people later hear what the storyer eliminated, or altered in the original telling.

***CRAFTED (EDITED) ORIGINAL TEXT***—Crafted original text stories have minimal crafting (editing & adaptation to oralize) to leave out or simplify confusing details (excessive proper names of minor characters, place names and non-essential numbers—especially large numbers) for less confusion and better focus for oral communicators and use in literacy programs for new readers. These deleted details add to the story "load" and, while appearing important to the storyteller, may compete with the storyline for comprehension and retention. Some limited light paraphrasing is permitted to express story portions with greater clarity in the storyer's own words, especially if simpler than the written verbatim text.

Compression of longer stories using bridging summaries to link the major story events has definite value. Brief inserts added for clarity in telling and understanding, substitution of proper names and nouns for pronouns to aid listeners' comprehension of dialog with who is speaking to whom are all helpful in story crafting. Where names are similar such as Elijah and Elisha some means of stereotyping one to distinguish it from the other where both appear in the same story, and where name changes occur like Abram to Abraham some story modification may be needed as name changes like this can be confusing, causing listeners to think of two different people, or for interpreters simply to use the same name all the way through a story. Pre-story comments to explain the differences in names or name changes can provide the needed understanding without having to insert explanation into the stories. Name changes are significant in many cultures, so this is not something necessarily to avoid.

In the Judges story of Ehud and Eglon, Dr. Grant Lovejoy suggests referring to "Ehud the left-handed" and "Eglon the fat" as a means of keeping the persons clearly identified by stereotyped descriptive terms. In the Elijah/Elisha stories it may be helpful to speak of "Prophet Elijah" and "Disciple Elisha" until Elijah is taken away into heaven and Elisha assumes the role as prophet and then becomes "Prophet Elisha." Many times I explained the different meaning of the two names to my interpreters so they would be prepared. Also I have stereotyped them as "old Prophet Elijah" and "young Prophet Elisha."

Vocabulary adjustment (*Israelites* instead called Abraham's *descendants*) as needed to reduce hostility or rejection of a story and its message by eliminating reactive story terminology can be helpful for Muslims. The object is to stay close as possible to the original Bible wording and storyline, yet sensitively make adjustment for clarity, story flow and reduction of distracting story elements. The many names or appellations for God and Jesus are confusing to some oral communicators.

As seen earlier, in some cultures (with Hindus especially) the use of the word "LORD" without further identifying "which" LORD can be a problem. In summary, only that which is essential to be changed for the sake of clarity and understanding, or to reduce hostility is altered in the basic story crafting.

*God and Woman*[18] and *Heaven Is For Women*[19] are examples of crafted stories in which an attempt was made to stay relatively close to the NIV wording in the model lessons with minimal rewording or summary narrative. Some minor rewording was needed to simplify or shorten longer stories. Some dialog references were altered for clarity for listeners.

*Advantages:* Crafted stories have definite value. One is retention of a relatively accurate story that is close to the Bible in wording. The gain in maintaining listener interest and receptivity, avoiding unnecessary hostility or rejection due to less important or reactive story elements, the possibility of enhanced comprehension are all positive factors. This method is a compromise between the verbatim and the paraphrased formats that retain some of the advantages of both without excessively compromising the accuracy of the story. Difference from Verbatim methodology lies mainly in degree of permitted crafting and the freedom to do as much as needed for clarity.

*Disadvantages:* This method also has disadvantages. Additions to a story in the form of comments may or may not be picked up by oral communicators in their retelling. Retention of dialog in crafting can increase difficulty for remembering and retelling.

Even this minimal crafting can pose difficulties for Muslims, especially if they later find that portions of the story were left out or "changed" as they might say. I have discovered that once believers are past the story of the Cross, some of these earlier story omissions and alterations in vocabulary can be understood as necessary in the original storytelling. For most listeners the gains outweigh what is lost in crafting if the stories tell well and are understood by listeners. In many cases reading the verbatim account first then allows one to "tell" the story in a more conversational language.

**COMPILED STORIES**—Compiled stories are crafted stories that are made up of component passages, all of which are found in the Bible and implied by the larger Bible story with possibly one exception of a story about the Bible that benefits from some extra-biblical comment. The compiled story itself, however, is not found in Scripture in a coherent form though the component parts suggest the compiled story when assembled together in a narrative. (Example: The Creation of the Spirit World which includes creation of angels as sinless, the work God gave them to do, the rebellion and fall of Satan and the punishment of evil spirits decreed in the coming judgment).

The purpose of The Creation of the Spirit World story is to condense into one basic narrative an understanding of God's sovereignty over the spirit world, that all God's work is righteous and without sin, and that God judges and will punish even the spirit world for their disobedience. It initially characterizes Satan and the evil spirits that will appear in later stories. The story is placed in an early chronological perspective as foundational, though parts of it are taken from the whole Bible.

Another example of a needed compiled story is that of the Bible and how it came to be. This requires some extra-biblical historical narrative as well as inclusion of selected narratives and Scripture passages that help listeners understand how God caused the Bible to be written and what it says about God's words. The purpose of this story is to introduce the Bible for those unfamiliar with it and to characterize and define it for those who have mistaken beliefs about the Bible. It is not to be a lecture on the Bible and its meaning.

Another example of a compiled story is one used to introduce the characteristics of God early in the storying chronology. Some typical versions are *The Living God* for Hindus and *The God Who Sees and Hears* for Muslim women. (This story is included in the chapter on women.)

The *Prophets' Story of the Messiah* is a compiled story used to transition from the Old Testament to the Gospel stories. The story draws on passages taken from Psalms, Isaiah (chapter 53 is the core passage), Micah, and Zechariah that tell of the Messiah's identity, place of birth and mother, what will happen to him, and what he will accomplish.

I have used a compiled biographical story of the disciple Peter that followed Peter from his first introduction to Jesus by Andrew through his ministry in Acts, mention in Paul's epistles and finally ending in the pastoral letters of Peter. Some of the stories of Paul may be compiled from Acts and references in the Epistles to give a coherent story related to what Paul wrote to the local believers in churches.

*Advantages:* The compiled story format provides a handy and usable means of introducing scriptural truth in a narrative format that is foundational or needed to give meaning to stories later on. Using compiled stories, the storyer finds special help in linking implied stories found in the Epistles where an Acts account and an Epistle

51

reference may be harmonized to suggest the story behind discipling truths. *The Story of the Bible* and *The Creation of the Spirit World* are foundational stories that are helpful early in a Bible Storying chronology.

*Disadvantages:* As to disadvantages, many persons are uncomfortable with "creating Bible stories" where they are not given as an intact, complete, and functional story found in one clearly defined location in Scripture. Interpretation of the passages in Isaiah 14 and Ezekiel 28, and possibly Revelation 12, may pose interpretation problems for some. One alternative suggested and used includes the *Job Story* to deal with the sovereignty of God (though it fails to deal with how Satan came to be). Another possibility is a compiled story of other references to the angels and evil spirits that still deal with God's creation and sovereignty over the spirits but specifically fail to deal with Satan's rebellion and the fact that he was created sinless and perfect "until wickedness was found in him." Some have used the *Witch of Endor* story to deal with evil spirits and those who practice communing with them.

**COMPOSITE STORIES** (Clustered Narratives, Extended Narratives, Enhanced Narratives)—Composite Stories are different from Compiled Stories in that whole or intact stories do exist. Clustering several intact stories that give different or focused perspective on a biblical truth can provide this focus. Clustered stories are generally related thematically or by characters and usually not chronologically. Many of the parables that the Gospel writers included are clusters of related stories with a common theme.

Clustered stories can also be used to depict contrast between good and evil or righteous and sinful, successful and failing characters and are helpful in oralizing discipleship and leadership stories.

Clustered stories are most commonly composed of several thematically-related or character-related stories joined together into a narrative grouping for greater impact and emphasis. All the stories in the cluster are told at the same time as a series of stories. Discussion usually follows the cluster.

Examples of clustered narratives the storyer can use are: the three parables of *The Lost Sheep*, *The Lost Coin*, and *The Lost (or Prodigal) Son* are a good example of thematically linked stories.

Many of the Kingdom of Heaven parables may be clustered as well as those of the *Wedding* and *Feast* parables, or the several stories dealing with obedience or being found faithful and ready for the Lord's return.

Stories about Jesus' forgiveness of sin such as *The Paralyzed Man and Four Friends, The Sinful Woman Who Anointed Jesus, Zacchaeus*, or *Jesus Forgives an Adulterous Woman*, driving out evil spirits as *The Demoniac in the Synagogue, The Gadarene Demoniac, The Boy with an Evil Spirit*, or *The Syro-Phoenician Woman's Daughter*, healing the sick, restoring the disabled, and raising the dead as in *Jairus' Daughter, Widow of Nain's Son, Raising of Lazarus* are examples of story clusters linked both by theme (raising to life) and character (Jesus).

Since these may come from different times in the chronology and may be arranged for a certain progression or impact, the timeline is generally ignored. In preparing discipleship and leadership track stories this clustering may be used to give greater emphasis to a particular spiritual truth and to provide several related examples of desirable characteristics and perspectives.

*Extended narratives* are juxtaposed individual stories that suggest or continue a storyline progression. Stories are extended by adding an entry story and one or more follow-through (or closure) stories. These include introductory stories that serve to prepare for the central story by introducing relationships that heighten the plot of the central story or give needed background. Follow-through stories then lead to resolution or some significant closure point. The stories are not created as in the Compiled Story but the existing component stories are simply pulled together with suitable bridging or combined into one extended narrative for greater effect.

Clustered stories are typically independent stories that share a common theme or teaching while providing differing perspectives or contrast. Extended stories form a series that introduces the main story and then might be followed by one or more closure stories.

A good example of an extended narrative is the story of David beginning with the narrative of David's desire for a drink from the well at Bethlehem where Uriah (Bathsheba's husband) is introduced along with Eliam (Bathsheba's father) in 2 Samuel 23. The story continues in 2 Samuel 11 with David's sin with Bathsheba, the plotted death of Uriah, David's prophetic reaction to Nathan's story, possibly inserts from Psalm 38 as confession of David's guilt and Psalm 51 as a cry for restoration of fellowship. Then following are the summarized stories of the deaths of four sons in fulfillment of David's prophetic accusation of the rich man in Nathan's story (David's love child, Amnon, Absalom, and Adonijah). The follow through stories serve to bring the main story to a very meaningful conclusion for those who live in cultures where their sons are their social security and the loss of a firstborn son is tragic, the loss of a beloved son is heartbreaking, and the death of still another son that desired the throne rounds out the fulfillment of David's prophetic judgment against himself.

Another Old Testament extended story might be *Naboth's Vineyard* that is preceded by a brief story of the Ten Commandments that defines sin and lists the Ten

Commandments including those that will be broken in the following story. Then the Naboth story from 2 Kings 21 and followed by brief accounts of the death of King Ahab from wounding in battle and of Jezebel's violent death in judgment of her sin.

The story of Jesus at the home of Mary and Martha provides another good example for beginning an extended narrative story. In some cultures, brother Lazarus should be mentioned for the story to be socially correct! The extended narrative can establish Jesus' relationship with the family of Mary and Martha (Luk 10), followed by the sickness, death, and raising of Lazarus (Jn 11), and in conclusion Mary's anointing of Jesus (Jn 12) for closure. Threads in these stories are Martha serving in the first and last story, and Mary giving her attention to Jesus also in the first and last story. Highlight of the main story are the testimonies of Jesus and Martha.

In the Old Testament the Abraham stories beginning with the *Sojourn in Egypt* provide material for an extended narrative for Muslims. The extended story begins with the visit to Egypt where Hagar was likely obtained as a servant, *Hagar's Pregnancy and Flight* and *Birth of Ishmael, The Sending Away of Ishmael*, and a wife from Egypt, listing of Ishmael's sons in fulfillment of God's promise make a series. Then for Isaac the story begins with God's telling Abraham that a son will come from his own body, *The Three Angelic Visitors, The Birth of Isaac*, and *The Substitute Sacrifice* make up an extended narrative. Stories of King Saul showing his spiritual highs and lows and final failure are examples of an extended biographic narrative. One Bible storyer in Japan made use of the extended biographical narrative of Moses that was popular with his youth listeners.

The linking of individual stories usually requires some narrative introduction to the series and minimal but appropriate bridging between stories to tie them together as a continuing developing story.

*Enhanced narratives* are illustrated in the story of the *Feeding the Five Thousand* in which details from the several Gospel accounts can be combined into one enhanced story. The *Annunciation* and *The Birth of Jesus* including the Luke and Matthew references can be an enhanced narrative that is also an extended narrative. Another possibility is the combining of details for the Last Supper in Luke, the post-supper discourse in John, prayer in the Garden, arrest and trial, Crucifixion and Resurrection stories of Jesus from the four Gospels.

A harmonized account of the four Gospels in *The Greatest Story*[20] is an example of taking the major (or longer) story account in the four Gospels and enhancing it with additional details taken from parallel accounts in the other three Gospels. The authors have taken the account with the most detail as the base account and added details from parallel Gospel accounts.

This same kind of harmonization is also provided in *The Story from the Book* where the kingdom and prophet stories are harmonized into combined stories, the four Gospels are similarly harmonized, and Acts and the Epistles are harmonized into combined single accounts. *The Story From the Book*[21] is a harmonized chronological narrative account of the Bible story edited into a shortened version that still retains the panoramic Redemption storyline.

Extended narratives are commonly used in fast-tracking a panorama of the *Redemption Story*. The enhanced fast-track narrative of *The Passion Story* brings together into one continuing narrative the rich details of the gathering hostility, the Last Supper, the post-supper discourse in John, the Garden prayer experience, the trials, Crucifixion with decisions for and against Jesus, and the Burial and Resurrection of Jesus. It is possible to enhance the *Creation Story* somewhat with passages from Job, Psalms, and Isaiah that relate to God's handiwork in Creation. The same is true for *The Creation of Man and*

*Woman* with various references particularly in Job and Psalm 8.

These various composite formatting options are not mutually exclusive but can be combined. These descriptive terms were chosen to describe the options that can be used for greater variety, emphasis, and utility in preparing Bible stories for telling.

*Advantages: Clustered narratives* heighten focus on a teaching theme by giving several perspectives from similar stories or a single magnified emphasis of the central theme. Clustered narratives can especially be used with stories characterizing Jesus as having the authority to forgive sin, authority over demons, power to heal illness and infirmity, authority over nature, and authority over death. Clustered narratives are also helpful in discipling and leadership storying tracks for theme emphasis.

*Extended narratives* provide opportunity for characters to develop in the story episodes as well as to follow a longer and larger story that is emerging. Also these narratives can establish needed relationships developing over several stories, provide important background, and show resolution or follow-through for the central story. Such series of stories can be significantly helpful for approaching delicate issues like the place of Ishmael in the Abraham story for Muslims and God's choice of Isaac as the son of promise.

*Enhanced narratives* provide deeper, richer story texture with collected details and story elements that are part of the same story but found in different accounts. They allow a more vivid or detailed story with greater interest and emotional impact. Enhanced narratives produce a harmonized account.

*Disadvantages:* The resulting composite stories may introduce too many details or be too complicated or long (as in extended stories) for listeners to remember the component stories and all their details easily. Oral communicators, unfamiliar with the Bible story, will generally accept these story formats as "Bible." There can be later problems when listeners become literate and try to find these stories as told in their Bible. So some explanation will be needed at that point. Some of the composite stories can affect the chronological timeline if that is an important organizational criteria.

**LIGHTLY PARAPHRASED STORIES**—This is a term I have used to describe rewording stories into simpler vocabulary, giving sharper focus to a story with elimination of distracting minor themes, and reorganizing the story for smoother flow. A lightly paraphrased story is more or less told in the storyteller's own words without significant expansion or altering the story as found in the Bible. A paraphrased story may be used to narrate some or all dialog rather than have characters speaking as this adds to complexity of story and slows the story down. Many children's stories are lightly paraphrased. This may be necessary for oral translations into a heart language where spiritual vocabulary is limited or minimal inserted comment is needed for clarity, and explanation of new or difficult-to-translate key term vocabulary.

One typical example of lightly paraphrased Bible stories would be *365 Short Stories From the Bible*[22]. The stories are fairly accurate but simplified for easy telling. Storying models based on *The Living Bible* or *Today's English Version* already have some element of paraphrasing in their stories. *The Story From the Book*[23] is another example of a lightly paraphrased chronological narrative account based on *The Book* (Living Bible).

Another value of paraphrased stories in the vernacular arises when the written text must be in a highly literate language due to cultural requirements, but high language is not the popular spoken language.

*Advantages:* Light paraphrasing generally speeds up the story by some use of summary, and limiting character dialog. Paraphrasing allows for some expansion of specific key parts of a story using additional descriptions that relate to the desired focus of the story, or enhance its comprehension. Paraphrasing allows putting a story into simpler language more suitable for telling. The storyline is not significantly altered in light paraphrasing.

*Disadvantages:* Light paraphrasing may introduce some loss of accuracy and authenticity where deep respect for Scripture exists or where a conservative oral Bible is part of strategy. Idiomatic expressions may not translate well or be understood by listeners in another culture. Stories learned in paraphrased form may conflict with stories obtained directly from the Bible when literacy comes. Advantages gained in comprehension and focus must be balanced against any relative long-term disadvantages.

**DEEPLY PARAPHRASED STORIES**—Deeply paraphrased stories involve significant reworking or rewording of a Bible story to work around difficult concepts that need careful explanation or expanding for comprehension. Some of these are deep compression of longer stories to serve as a summary bridge between stories of major importance in a Bible Storying strategy, significant expansion through use of additional descriptive words and phrases to heighten impact by describing locations or characters in greater detail, preparing listeners by providing enhanced (and perhaps more relevant) visualization of the story. Examples of paraphrased Bible stories in story sets are *God and Man*[24] and *Chronological Bible Storytelling—54 Bible Stories*[25]. Both of these early models made use of deeply paraphrased stories.

*Advantages:* This method possesses strong theme development possibilities. Often this approach provides more interesting stories for listeners, especially in those stories that lack an active, rapidly moving plot and interaction between characters. This method also provides a means of loading more teaching into the story narrative itself. The summarized form becomes very useful for bridging stories where details are not needed at the moment, but only an outline story to maintain some form of continuity between major stories that are needed for teaching.

*Disadvantages:* Deeply paraphrased stories can suffer loss of accuracy for those not knowing the story from the Bible. It does not fit oral Bible strategy because of the liberties taken in crafting. Considerable teaching can be included in the formatting of the story, thus blurring the difference between story and teaching from the story. The method can unwittingly introduce new elements or focus to a story not intended in the original wording.

**RECAST STORIES**—Recast stories constitute a resetting of Bible stories to preserve the basic plot and spiritual/moral teaching, but to alter the details of the original story for any of several reasons like increasing relationship to listeners or avoiding troublesome issues. An example of increasing relationship with Muslims is a recasting of the *Parable of Two Men Who Went Into the Temple to Pray* (Luk 18) that begins: "There were two Muslim men who went into a mosque to pray..."[26] *The Parable of the Prodigal Son* is a story often recast into other cultures or characters. Consider a version of *The Prodigal Daughter* as relating to young women and their need for repentance and forgiveness. Stories on forgiveness may draw on biblical stories while being recast into local cultures. Recast stories can be used to relationally introduce the biblical teaching. The biblical source story should always be told after the recast story.

*Advantages:* To increase perceived relevance and relationship, and for certain instances among a hostile people, a recasting into another time, place or people may eliminate national and other references which could alienate listeners. The recast story plot usually parallels the original Bible story though characters, location, and actual story plot may vary somewhat. The recast story has advantages for use among literates who can read the source story but may need the recast story in order to connect.

*Disadvantages:* The recast story may not be recognized as a Bible story. Recasting may introduce new and unwanted elements. Where a recast story is used in conjunction with a biblical story there is danger of confusion of which is the true story. Creating such confusion is definitely out of bounds for oral Bible strategies.

**DRAMATIZED STORIES**—This format can be an accurate dramatization of the Bible story, keeping close to the biblical account, or it may have more of the nature of a recast story. The main difference between a recast story and a recast story drama is the acting out or visualization of the story. Dramatized stories have value in media presentations and in dealing with certain worldview issues that benefit from being explored dramatically.

*Advantages:* Generally dramatized stories have interest and entertaining value for the audience. Dialog may range anywhere from verbatim with role-playing to adlibbing. Usually additional dialog is needed for silent characters and actions added to enhance and visualize drama. In the story of Peter and John's healing the cripple in Acts 3, John has no dialog in the Bible account; this would be needed for a drama.

Dialog and acting slow the story down so a dramatized story would typically be longer than a told story. Emotional impact is higher than for a story that is simply narrated. Teaching is heightened as the listeners relate to characters and internalize the visualized theme or spiritual teaching the story depicts. Dramatized stories are a cost effective means of illustrating Bible stories over using costly imported picture sets or other media. Drama is participative giving opportunity for characters to learn and act out the story plot. Drama by local people reduces alienation of stories that happened in other cultures.

*Disadvantages:* Outside of whatever modification of the Bible story is needed, the dramatic interpretation by actors may give different focus than the original story conveys, and introduce new and unwanted emphases. Dramatized stories should always be accompanied by properly told Bible stories, usually before the drama is presented to illustrate the narrated story.

***CHANTED OR SUNG STORIES***—Poetic chanting is a popular form of telling longer stories in many cultures. Stories are formed into a poetic rhyming meter that is then chanted with or without participatory refrains joined by the listeners. There is often repetition of key phrases that serve to highlight the theme of the passages. Among the Kui of Orissa, India, the *das kata* storytelling format is a form of rhythmic narration and sung intervals accompanied by clicking two sticks together.

On one occasion in Chacheungsao, Thailand a rural pastor began chanting the book of Genesis in a poetic rhythm. He said that form of recounting the Bible was popular among his people. When listeners stopped him after about ten minutes, he assured them that he could chant the whole of Genesis!

Sung stories are easier to remember and lend themselves quite well to recall while listeners are performing their daily tasks. Many cultures use music to preserve important events and to instruct rising generations. Sung stories are often a part of folk art presentations in which drama, narration, and song are intermixed into familiar and stirring presentations. In one south Asian country a type of cantata consisting of narrated story, drama, and songs telling the story of Jesus has been used successfully among Muslims who welcome the cultural aspect and accept the biblical message in that format.

Story songs are usually in one of two formats. One is more of a ballad style in which the song tells the story in a condensed form. It is generally performed by a person for the benefit of listeners. The other style consists of verses that tell either portions of a story or recall some characteristics of a person or God. A chorus then sums up the general theme. In some instances listeners will join the chorus or refrain.

An interesting event happened in the West Africa nation of Togo. A missionary and her pastor were upcountry among the Ife people where she was telling Bible stories. While doing so, the missionary noticed that her pastor was busily engaged writing something and apparently not listening to her stories. When she finished the stories, she chastised her pastor for not giving his undivided attention and support while she told the Bible stories. He just smiled and then asked if she knew what he was doing. As it turned out the pastor was listening to the stories and writing story songs for the people. He replied that it was good that the missionary was telling the stories because she did not sing very well! As I recall over 100 scripture songs were composed in that area.

*Advantages:* Story songs are very popular among the typical rural or tribal listeners as both entertaining and memorable. This format may overcome hostility among those whose worldview is seriously challenged by the Bible stories in that the cultural form of chanting or music reduces the foreignness of the story.

*Disadvantages:* Composing story songs is a nearly impossible task for an outsider to learn and do in a culturally acceptable manner. Use would depend upon patient teaching of a gifted or designated person within the culture who could then format the Bible stories into the chanted form or song. While in New Mexico I heard a Navajo pastor sing a brief song about the return of Jesus. Many of his radio listeners were attracted to this song and its message.

**INTERRUPTED NARRATIVES**—It is with fear and trembling that interrupted narratives are even included as a possible storytelling format. It is, in my opinion, anathema for oral communicators to have their stories interrupted while the storyteller pauses to insert some teaching that is extracted from the previous story fragment before the interruption. Still this format is used by some in which the story is paused at some pre-determined breaking points and the listeners put on hold while the storyteller discharges extracted truth. It can work in certain circumstances after there is familiarity with the story being told so that the listeners already know how the story continues and finishes. Still it is a literate practice and almost never observed among oral communicators unless influenced by Western teaching. Even then the local storyteller may go through the motions as they have learned from an outside teacher, but the intended effect is largely lost on the listeners who may consider the several parts of the interrupted story as different stories when the storyer continues.

The greatest case for doing this might be for use in longer extended narratives like the Joseph story, the Hezekiah story, or even in some circumstances in the stories of Jesus or Paul, or possibly for discipling tracks. I will admit to hearing an interrupted longer story where it was periodically paused for listeners to sing and relax mentally before the story continued. When I was telling a panorama of the Bible story to oral leaders I had to pause from time to time to allow my listeners to "rest" mentally and sometimes emotionally by singing a song before continuing the story.

Interrupted narratives are an extreme case not to be confused with brief comments that need inserting to clarify unfamiliar story elements. Those story elements are part of the story. The truly interrupted narrative is related to the teacher's need to extract truths that are contained or implied in the preceding story fragment. This practice is on the borderline between true Bible Storying

64

and just Bible Teaching. In the antecedent to the revival of Bible Storying the Bible story was referred to as the source of the teaching. But the story itself was seldom told or taught as a coherent story while expositional teaching served to unpack the story for listeners. Teaching from the story is a highly efficient way of packaging information drawn from the story, but a highly inefficient means of communicating that information to oral communicators. Literates who already know the stories may enjoy getting to the organized story truths or bottom line without having to hear the story again. Then again even literates can enjoy hearing the story told without interruption.

*Advantages:* These interrupted stories would be reassuring for the Bible teacher who is overly concerned that listeners who only hear an uninterrupted story without the associated teaching comments will miss something important. It could also be for those highly literate who know the stories well and want to get to the "real meat" in the stories that can be extracted and organized in an oral outline.

*Disadvantages:* Definitely the interrupted narrative holds a disadvantage for the oral communicator with the worst case being one who is hearing the interrupted story for the first time, and unfamiliar with how the story proceeds. It is conceivable that such a person could see the teaching "as part of the story" which is very difficult to remember and retell without notes. Also it is possible that story fragments could each be considered as independent stories that may or may not make sense in their fragmentary state.

In conclusion, all of these various story formats may be presented live directly to listeners in person, via radio as pre-recorded story programs, on audiocassette or other digital media. The characteristics of the medium, the allotted time, and other factors can influence which format is best. Generally it will be one of the verbatim formats or the crafted or lightly paraphrased format. This writer prefers the middle ground of the crafted or oralized stories doing only what is absolutely needed to make a Bible story understandable, memorable and retellable by oral learners.

# Chapter 7

## Guidelines For
## Oralizing Stories

Following are some guidelines for crafting Bible stories that you may consider using in preparing to tell them. You will likely choose one of the first several formats, either initially or later by default, as you begin to tell Bible stories. You do need to give this some thought and prayer as you begin to prepare the Bible stories which are the *heart* of the Bible Storying Session.

1. *First be sure you understand the story yourself.* Read the story as often as needed until you know it well. I suggest that a story be read anywhere from four to ten times. Read it aloud! You *hear* the story better when reading aloud. As you read the story, gesture and pause, and change your expression to emphasize the story. This helps you to internalize the story. Examine the story to visualize where it takes place, study who the characters are and their relationships, think about what explanation or story should precede or lead into the main story, what is the plot of the story with its scenes, the sequence of major plot events, subplots, and the outcome or resolution of the story? What did the story teach? Try to imagine why this story was originally told or included in the Bible. What might its moral or main theme(s) be in that day and today? What minor themes are also in the story? How might the story be understood or misunderstood by your listeners? What will your listeners likely relate to or like about the story? What will be difficult for listeners?

   Consider at what point will you begin (or enter) the story and how will you end (stop or reach a closure point) the story?

Some stories are rich in themes like *The Flood Story*: the omniscience of God (seeing both evil and good), the righteous judgment of God, the mercy of God (delay of the flood for 120 years), the grace of God (revealing to Noah how to save his family and animals), obedience leading to salvation (three times it is stated that Noah did everything God commanded him to do), the provision of salvation in the form of the ark, God's remembering those being saved from the flood after the judgment had passed, the thanksgiving sacrifice, the promise of God never to destroy the earth again by water, the permission to eat meat with the warning to remove the lifeblood, and finally the commandment to replenish the population of the earth.

You'll probably tell the story the first time with a primary focus on God's inescapable judgment of sin and a secondary focus on God's grace and Noah's obedience resulting in salvation. Later, provision of salvation in the time of judgment and salvation through obedience would be the primary focus in your discipling affirmation lessons. You will do more to explore these themes in the pre and post-story dialog time, but you need to consider this in crafting the story.

*The Flood Story* is a long story with many details in it that the storyer will likely want to streamline a bit. We will consider more on this later. First, learn to ferret out the story themes and identify the major theme(s) that are your reason for using that story.

2. *Pause to pray about the story, asking for wisdom to understand the story and its meaning and implication for listeners and why you have chosen this story.* This prayer sometimes is for the best decision among several possible stories. The answer may not come until you actually begin working on the stories and the Holy Spirit guides you about which is best to use and

how to tell it. I've chosen stories from my logic but the Holy Spirit indicated a different story to use.

3. *Visualize the story and the characters in it.* After you have read the story several times and are familiar with it, close your eyes and see the story as you listen to the characters speaking and moving. This vision will help you capture the setting and flow of the story as you prepare it.

Pay attention to the clues that identify characters. Can you "see" the characters? Describe them. Use descriptives that stereotype the characters. In Judges 3, Ehud is left-handed and Eglon King of Moab is very fat. Saul was a "head taller than others" when he was anointed king. Rahab was a prostitute but also a very pro-active woman. Elijah wore a leather girdle (or belt) and coarse clothing of camel's hair. Zacchaeus was a short man.

There are basically three kinds of characters in a story—round, flat, and stock.[27]

a. *Round characters* are like "real people" who possess a variety of traits, some of which may even conflict, so the behavior is not always predictable. Jesus and the disciples count as round characters as they possess many traits like real people. Did Jesus act "out of character" with the Syro-Phoenician woman? What about Jesus' sly replies to the trick questions brought to accuse him? The disciples especially are round characters as they express many conflicting traits throughout the stories: faith, fear, doubt, excitement, boldness, and jealousy. Naaman the leper went from being a proud and angry leper to a humbled and generous healed man.

b. *Flat characters* in contrast have few traits and act predictably. The religious leaders, Pharisees and Judas are flat characters with predictable roles.

Pharaoh in the Plagues stories is seen to be flat as he settles into a predictable behavior.

c. *Stock characters* are those who possess only one trait and are minor actors in the stories. The leper in Mark 1 exhibits a single trait of faith. Other stock characters are those in the crowds who followed Jesus, enjoying his teaching, and were especially pleased when Jesus put the Pharisees and religious leaders in their place.

4. *Look for stereotypes and irony in stories.* In the Gospel stories of Jesus the Pharisees and religious leaders take on a stereotypical role—always sneering, criticizing, and posing difficult questions to trap Jesus.

Irony in stories is when the good is bad and the bad is good, or there is an unusual twist of fate at the end that is unsuspected. There is irony in the story of Nicodemus as he is out of character with other Pharisees and defends Jesus in a later encounter when the Pharisees are judging Jesus unfairly. In *The Parable of the Good Samaritan* the hated Samaritan is the good person and the bad persons are the religious leaders who fail to stop and render aid to the wounded traveler. The woman who had lived a sinful life and came to anoint the feet of Jesus was said to have provided the hospitality that Simon the self-righteous Pharisee host had failed to do.

5. *Be aware of things in the story that may culturally or socially offend,* and might therefore, stop further listening, draw attention away from the central theme, or leave a confusing thought. Two earlier examples come to mind. First is the story of Deborah and Barak in Judges 4-5 that ends with Sisera entering the tent of Jael who was alone. Jael extended initial hospitality to Sisera and then killed him while he slept. In some cultures this double-edged sword will cut two ways—Sisera did a bad thing because Jael's husband was not present; Jael did a bad thing

because anyone under someone's roof is traditionally under their protection in the Middle Eastern cultures.

Another earlier example is the story of *Jesus and the Samaritan Woman* in John 4. In the story, the account mentions that the disciples left Jesus to go into the town to buy food. Then the woman came alone to the well and Jesus spoke to her. In many cultures this is a very bad scene with a woman who is later found to have a bad reputation being alone with a holy man who is not family or her husband. So in crafting this story for those people, the part about the disciples leaving Jesus alone to be met by the woman could be omitted in telling the story until listeners have a better understanding of who Jesus is.

Incidentally, a storying trainer can't tell the storyer what to do or not do. Guidelines come from past experiences primarily of the trainer, but also shared from those who network with him. Pray about all things, but especially about making decisions affecting the story content and format for telling.

6. *Be aware that stories that offend or embarrass you may be acceptable stories for others.* A classic example of this is the story of Jephthah and the implied fate of his daughter who came out to meet him after his victory (Jdg 10-11). I have never personally liked that story but found it was a good story among a people where honor was an important worldview issue. These people viewed the story in an entirely different light, seeing the daughter honor her father by apparently submitting to death, so he could in turn honor God by keeping his vow. I had to learn to craft and tell that story without revealing my personal distaste for it. Interestingly, that story was a good foundational story for that of Jesus who honored his Father by submitting even to death and was in turn honored by God by being raised to life again and raised to the right hand of power.

Other examples might be stories like that of Jacob with his four wives (Rachel and Leah and the two concubines Bilhah and Zilpah) or David or Solomon and their many wives. The aim is not to let your personal distaste for a story affect the crafting and use of the story if it is applicable to your listeners.

7.  *Consider where to begin the story and how to end it.*
    An example is *The Cain and Abel story*. I have struggled with whether to mention God's mark on Cain as this raises a question about what the mark is, but decided to keep it in as it is another instance of God's grace toward Cain. The story that follows of Cain's descendant who killed someone who wounded him may or may not contribute to the basic story. A possible ending for the Cain and Abel story is to skip down to God's granting another son to replace Abel and that he (Seth) and his son exhibited a godly trait of calling on the name of the Lord. So read the larger passage and decide where to enter your story and where to end it with closure.

    In the same manner *The Flood Story* needs to end on a positive note with the rainbow and promise where there is closure. The post-story of Noah's drunkenness and cursing of Canaan may have later value in a discipling or leadership track of stories.

    In *The Flood Story* it may be best to begin the oral story past the first part of the account of the sons of God and daughters of men, unless you plan to explain this beforehand. While this incident leads into the main story, it is in itself a separate story that can raise questions the main story does not directly address and can divert listeners from the major story of judgment and obedience.

    *The Destruction of Sodom and Gomorrah* story has the sordid ending of Lot's daughters each sleeping with their father to have a child. This introduces a new thought that may distract listeners from the judgment of the Sodomites and salvation grace expressed to Lot and his family in the main story. Now if the theme of the story is about Lot and his family then you can explore the wife's reluctance to leave her people in the city and the two daughters' desire not to be left childless after the deaths of their future husbands in the destruction of the cities.

In the Elijah story of *The Sacrifice on Mount Carmel* there are several scenes depending on where you choose to begin the story. If the story of *The Widow of Zarephath* is omitted for the moment, the story could begin with the drought and God's care for Elijah, or it could begin with Elijah meeting Obadiah who in turn sets up the meeting with King Ahab. Then the story shifts to the top of Mount Carmel and has at least three scenes there: the pagan altar and priests' ritual, God's altar with Elijah's prayer and God's response and the people's response and confession, and the resolving scene of the coming rain to break the drought.

8. *Keep the dialog if at all possible* for two reasons. One is that much of the interest for listeners is in overhearing the story characters speak to one another. A second reason is that sometimes the characters can say things in a safer, more acceptable way that might be too confrontational if coming directly from the storyteller as comment or teaching. That way you the storyteller can remain neutral with some distancing from hard-to-accept truths, and still maintain the relationship with the listeners as storyteller. For instance, allow the many testimonies from story characters saying that Jesus is the Son of God. In that way it is not you the storyer saying it, but the people in the stories are saying it.

Dialog carries much of the emotion expressed in a story—joy, confrontation and anger, amazement, fear, and devotion. Think of Ruth's story without the poignant dialog between Ruth and Naomi and the tender dialog between Ruth and Boaz. Check out King Saul's dialog in 1 Samuel 20:30-31. Remember that dialog slows a story down, making the story longer and more complicated to tell and remember, but dialog adds life and interest to the story. Listeners enjoy overhearing story characters speaking and often can relate to them through the dialog.

9. *The Bible uses adjectives sparingly* to describe people and places. Adjectives also slow stories down and too many can lead to clutter rather than clarity. Well-chosen simple adjectives or descriptive phrases (often of a concrete relational nature like similes and metaphors) may say more than a string of many colorful adjectives.

10. *The Bible uses summary statements and narrators' comments.* Genesis 25:34b has a pithy comment regarding Esau. See also the comments made about the kings of Israel and Judah—2 Kings 15:12; 2 Chronicles 29:2. Use these summary statements and narrators' comments.

11. *Decide on the name you will use for God and be consistent in using it.* God is not His name but is a descriptive of who He is. With Muslims you will probably just use Allah in every instance except where a compound descriptive name is used. This may already be decided in the Bible translation used. In other cultures it will be necessary to be consistent but at the same time sure that the name used is not confused with local deities. Among Hindus it is not sufficient to say "the LORD" as listeners may put in their own "lord." As we understood earlier it must be the "LORD Jehovah," the "Lord Jesus," etc. Switching back and forth between "the LORD" and other names

can be confusing to oral communicators listening to a story, so be consistent. Most oral peoples relate better to a name than to a description. The exception to this appears to be the practice among Native Americans who tend to use descriptive names as a form of stereotyping story characters. God may be simply called "Creator." Adam would be "first man."

12. *For some nonliterates it is helpful to limit new proper names of people and places in the stories.* A literacy worker in Malawi has suggested a limit of three. More proper names can be used if the characters or location are familiar and known from previous stories. In the story of King Saul's offering the sacrifice in 1 Samuel 13, the Philistines might simply be "the enemy." In the story of the anointing of David as the next king the names of the brothers who stood before the Prophet Samuel are not needed for the story to make sense. Samuel, Jesse, and David are the principle characters. Of course, in the story of the "birth wars" of Leah, Rachel, and the two maidservants, the names of the twelve sons and daughter are important as the meaning of the names for each is given. Even if listeners do not remember all the names, they generally enjoy the story and its pathos and humor and may remember the names as well.

13. *On very short stories look for ways to extend the story* by giving some background or a bridging story leading into it. In this way the very short story might be framed by a larger story or sandwiched between a bridging story and a closure story. An example is that of the two Hebrew midwives in Exodus 1:15-21. The story may be lengthened by adding the part about the new king of Egypt and the oppression leading up to the order to kill the boy babies. No doubt their action also saved the life of infant Moses at his birth.

14. *On very long stories it may help to break the story up into scenes and use some mnemonic device* in telling

the story to help listeners follow and remember the story. Some do this by staging the story as they change positions (or enact the scene) in telling the story. Use extra care in crafting these longer stories to keep them simple, flowing, and well organized. But don't be afraid to use them. Examples are: Ruth, Esther, Joseph, Jonah, and others like Hezekiah.

15. *Also in the case of long stories with numerous episodes like the Joseph story consider breaking the longer story down into several shorter stories that focus on one truth or teaching point.* Some storyers have used cliffhangers to lead up to a dramatic point and stop, to be followed by the conclusion story later. Abraham's preparation to sacrifice his son Isaac has been told in this manner. However, in one account from the early days of Chronological Bible Teaching a well-meaning teacher told the story of the trial and crucifixion of Jesus and stopped at the burial saying, "Tomorrow we will continue the story." It was later told that some of the fierce listeners told the teacher, "No, you will finish the story now!"

16. *Pay attention to "verbal threads" and story pacing.* Verbal threads[28] are repetitions in stories that link parts of the story. In the Resurrection story of the women there are three threads in the story structure of Mark 16: "they were on their way to the tomb" (v. 2), "As they entered the tomb" (v. 5), and "the women went out and fled from the tomb" (v. 8). This thread introduces each of the women's movements and links parts of the story. In *The Flood Story* the remark is made three times that Noah did all that God commanded him (Gen 6:22; 7:5; 7:16). In the story of *Three Men and the Fiery Furnace* there is a rhythm in the repetition of the musical instruments four times in the story (Dan 3:5, 7, 10, 15). Threads serve to link story parts and can serve to impart an interesting rhythm in the telling.

17. *Consider adding in nouns and proper names in place of pronouns, especially in the Gospel stories.* For example read in Luke 24 the story of the women who came to the tomb to anoint the body of Jesus. In verse 1 the women are identified. In verses 2-4 the women are referred to as "they" or as "them." It is not until verse 5 that again they are identified as "the women." Then it is not again until verse 11 that they are identified as "the women."

Following is another example of changes that may be helpful for your listeners and interpreters if used. First, read Mark 3:1-6 in your Bible noting how many pronouns are used in telling this story. Think about your interpreter, if used, or your listeners who are trying to follow the story and who is saying or doing what to whom. Then read the oralized where the pronouns have been replaced with proper names or nouns. Italics indicate the replaced words.

1 Another time *Jesus* went into the synagogue, and a man with a shriveled hand was there.
2 Some of *the people* were looking for a reason to accuse Jesus, so *the people* watched *Jesus* closely to see if *Jesus* would heal *the man* on the Sabbath.
3 Jesus said to the man with the shriveled hand, "Stand up in front of everyone."
4 Then Jesus asked *the people*, "Which is lawful on the Sabbath: to do good or to do evil, to save life or to kill?" But *the people* remained silent.
5 *Jesus* looked around at *the people* in anger and, deeply distressed at *the people's* stubborn hearts. Jesus said to the man, "Stretch out your hand." *The man* stretched out his hand, and *the man's* hand was completely restored.
6 Then the Pharisees went out and began to plot with the Herodians how they might kill Jesus.

I realize that it gets tiresome for a literate to repeat all the nouns and proper names, but it can be very helpful to an interpreter and especially helpful for listeners to keep track of what is happening. This

77

takes some getting used to, but after doing it for several stories, it becomes very natural.

18. On a similar note *it is very helpful to name who is speaking to whom in character dialog*. This suggestion accompanies the replacement of pronouns with nouns and proper names. Ex: Jesus said to his disciples, "…". The disciples replied to Jesus, "…". Read Mark 8:27-30 the incident of Peter's confession of Jesus. Following is the same passage with the speakers and listeners identified in the dialog quotes (added words in italics):

27 Jesus and his disciples went on to the villages around Caesarea Philippi. On the way *Jesus* asked *the disciples*, "Who do people say I am?"

28 *The disciples* replied, "Some say John the Baptist; others say Elijah; and still others, one of the prophets."

29 "But what about you? Who do you say that I am?" Jesus asked his disciples. Peter answered, "You are the Christ."

30 Jesus warned *the disciples* not to tell anyone about *who Jesus was*.

Also *it can be helpful to keep character dialog quotes unbroken*. From time to time the Bible translators will allow Jesus to begin speaking, then identify him as the speaker, then continue his words. Notice in verse 29 above that I joined the two questions of Jesus without the speaker identifying phrase interrupting. In Mark 10:35 James and John make a request of Jesus:

"Teacher," they said, "we want you to do for us whatever we ask."

Consider revising to:

James and John said to Jesus, "Teacher, we want you to do for us whatever we ask."

19. *Short sentences increase the tempo of a story.* Longer sentences slow the tempo. Adjectives and dialog slow the tempo of a story, verbs speed up the tempo. Look

at the use of verbs in Genesis 25:34—*gave, ate, drank, got up*, and *left*.

20. *The Church Planting and Characterization Track stories require more creativity* as some of these stories are composite stories or may have several components from different passages. The breaking of bread referenced in Acts 2:42 might be linked to the institution of the Passover in Exodus 12-13 and the Last Supper in Luke's Gospel showing that the believers were remembering the death of Jesus just as they had remembered the Passover from the days in Egypt.

21. *Limit geographical place names to those absolutely necessary for the story.* Obviously "Bethlehem" is essential in the *Birth of Jesus* narrative. In 1 Samuel 13 quite a number of places are named which can leave the listeners bewildered as to what these words mean. The places are Micmash, Bethel, Gibeah of Benjamin, Geba, Gilgal, Beth Aven, Jordan, Gad and Gilead. Several places are named in the stories of Abraham. Some are however significant to the stories and need to be named, especially if related to some story event that happened there.

22. *Use the best level of language for crafting the story.* I've already mentioned the matter of some cultures having a high language that is usually required for holy writings, and may be common in most literature including the local Bible. This is not the language that people normally speak. If the target listeners tell their stories in vernacular or common language, then they probably understand that language best. Jesus taught in vernacular or spoken language, not in literary Hebrew. This procedure is not always easy and a compromise may be necessary for some listeners who are more literate and are able to read from the written text. However, even a literate listener may have trouble with their own high language.

23. *Explain unusual or unknown items in the story outside the story.* To keep the story uninterrupted in telling and understandable, plan to explain any needed background items before beginning the story. Sometimes it is possible to add on the necessary background story as a bridging story, telling it and then going right into the main story. An example would be the *Resettlement of Samaria* in 2 Kings 17 before either *The Parable of the Good Samaritan* or *Jesus and the Samaritan Woman* stories. Other minor things may be handled with an aside like John did in *The Wedding at Cana* story when he commented on the water pots "... the kind used by the Jews for ceremonial washing..."

24. *Write out the story as you will tell it.* Remember to write it for *talking* and not for *reading*! Read the story aloud. Does it read well? Can you tell it without using your notes? I have said to write out the story as you will tell it. In some circumstances I have found it helpful *not* to put the story into writing, to retain the freedom and interpretation that only an oral preparation can give.

    I am sharing these guidelines for those who may need first to write out a story as they would tell it. If you don't need to do this, then you don't have to do it. Many oral storying models exist that did not go through the process of being first written out as crafted stories but were simply oralized when they were learned.

25. *Write out the story if it is to be shared with other users.* After the story is crafted orally, it can be written out as crafted, and saved to pass along to others who are literate and prefer to obtain stories in written format. Many early story sets were oral models in that the selection of stories and crafting of stories led to an oral-only model that was simply

remembered and told from memory. *The Suffering Servant*[29] model for Bengali Muslims existed as an oral-only model for a number of years before a new missionary couple asked for a written English version.

The down side of this occurs when a story is crafted in English and then simply translated into the listeners' language without using the English crafting as only a model to suggest possible crafting in the listeners' own language. The *God and Man* stories were originally prepared as paraphrases in the Ilongot tribal language of the Philippines, and then back translated into English. Many early storyers took the English back-translated paraphrase and from it translated the stories into still another language. Instead, the English stories in *God and Man* should have only been used as a suggested model for a new translation from English or whatever source Bible language is used.

As I write this I am counselling a storyer who is adding Bible stories to a set of lessons she has already prepared and been using. She wrote to ask if it were okay to record her telling the stories after she learned them and then to transcribe the oral stories into written form for her lesson book. I suggested that if it is the best way to prepare her stories, then she should do it. Of course, she can touch up the written account if needed for others as a model.

26. *Test the crafted story by reading it aloud for feel and flow.* Read it or tell to a person who will be honest in evaluating the story as a told story. Revise as needed. Or record the story, wait a day or so, and listen to it critically. The longer the wait, the better the review as it gives time for the story to fade a bit in your mind.

27. *Test the crafted story with a trusted informant for any vocabulary, grammatical, or plot structure that is unclear.* Can the informant retell the story to you?

How well does it return? Are there any places where the retelling stumbles or is uncertain?

Are there certain storytelling protocols followed among listeners which if not followed may discredit a Bible story? There are some societies where the moral of the story is announced before the story is told. Other protocols may call for certain rhythms to be established in the story or allowance made for refrains or responses by the listeners. You should know this from the worldview and culture study before beginning a Bible Storying strategy.

28. *When finished with crafting and polishing, use the story with your listeners.* Get multiple retellings from them if possible. If there are any rough spots in your telling or their retelling, look at any necessary revision in the crafting. My own rule of thumb is that it takes 2-3 storying sessions for my stories to settle down and stabilize and this allows for corrections or revisions related to listener response.

29. *Once a story crafting style is established, continue to use it for all the stories in that package, realizing that some variation in format may be needed for certain stories, though the general presentation style of telling can be retained.* Watch for clues and subtle shifts in how the stories are retold both in the storying sessions and, if possible, to be present when listeners are retelling the stories on other occasions. Watch for changes and any difficulties and either additions or omissions listeners make to the stories.

30. *When stories are crafted for radio, audiocassette or digital media, the storyteller is working blind from the listeners and cannot immediately know their response.* It is important to anticipate listener response when crafting the stories for even greater simplicity in the recorded medium and to allow for response pauses when recording the stories. It may be helpful to record

the stories before a small group of listeners who are your proxy audience so you can see their response.

One advantage of audiocassette or digital recordings of stories is that they can be replayed over and over again for complex stories that need a second or third hearing for understanding. Broadcast stories cannot be replayed so must be simpler and less complex. For audiocassette media the length of stories is not overly critical unless stories are being played on hand-cranked players. Experience has indicated that no story should exceed about five minutes maximum in this case. For radio presentation stories and whatever pre-story introduction and post-story teaching must fit a predetermined time frame.

A 15-minute program would typically have time for one story and any pre and post-story comments or rhetorical questions. A 30-minute program allows for multiple stories, but is easy to overload listeners with too much information at one time. A single story told and dramatized would be a better choice for interest and retention. The story should always be primary and prepared first before proceeding with the introductory and post-story parts of the program. It is usually helpful to have the same voice tell the stories each time and for that voice to be separate from any narrator who provides the introduction or teaching. This helps to set the story apart aurally for the listeners.

31. *Stories for children will need to be simplified appropriately using simple language and limited story details.* Short verbatim stories can be used or light paraphrasing of longer stories may be needed.

32. *Remember that a story is a story and not simply a narrative report of what happened.* Study it as a story and think of it as really happening as it will be told. Balance the crafted story between verbatim accuracy

and being a good oral story that will be told to listeners so that they can experience it, understand it and retell it.

33. *If possible, work with your interpreters in crafting Bible stories for telling.* Read or tell the verbatim story to your interpreter and then ask how they would retell it for their people. This dynamic working together will help you to put the story into a format for comprehension by the listeners and will help to prepare your interpreter to faithfully convey the told story to listeners with minimum misunderstanding. I suggest reading the verbatim story and then have the interpreter to read it verbatim in their language. Then tell the crafted story in English and work out any needed changes. Defend the crafting and tell why you did it. But be sensitive to the interpreter's suggestions for a smooth interpretation. By doing this you are helping the interpreter to learn the story.

Conclusion: These have been suggested guidelines and not rules to follow blindly. A well-crafted story is one that tells well, is durable so that it holds up when passing through interpretation, and is received and understood by listeners, remembered, and can be accurately retold. Pay close attention to how listeners retell the stories and learn from them. Your interpreter and listeners are your teachers. You want God's Story that you have prepared as your story to be their story.

# Chapter 8

## Oralizing Stories for Children

I have kept the subject of crafting Bible stories for children separate. Many of the same guidelines apply when preparing Bible stories for telling to children as for adult oral learners. It is not necessary to "dumb down" Bible stories for children because you think they can't handle complex stories. Children do have very active imaginations and can easily surprise storyers in what they can understand, retain, and retell.

If I were to choose one consideration for a focus, I would choose the worldview consideration for the child's mind and heart. I always counsel Bible storyers that Bible stories are "adult" stories and not children's stories just because they are stories. The Bible stories deal with adult themes and many are brutally honest in how the stories progress and turn out where sin and judgment are involved.

One of my colleagues was telling about his daughter who had been exposed to an adult version of the *David and Goliath* story at home. In the story as she heard it and knew it, after David had struck down Goliath, David took Goliath's own sword and cut off the giant's head. Apparently the girl's Sunday school teacher in an effort to make the story more suitable for children ended her story more kindly for the giant. As I recall hearing about the incident, the daughter may have corrected her teacher for not telling the story correctly, and may have added in the real ending. Children can handle gruesome details in the stories!

But sometime the opposite is true. Once in a Kui tribal village in India I was using an evangelistic preaching poster that told a fictional story of a man who had a dream in which he was being pursued by a fearsome tiger. The tiger represented the man's sins. In the dream the tiger relentlessly pursued the man who was attempting to outrun the tiger to escape the consequences of his sin. Each time the man would hide; the tiger would soon find him again. At last the man came to a precipice and could therefore run no farther. He heard the tiger coming and knew he could not escape. But just then the man saw two vines hanging over the edge and the man quickly reached for the vines and began climbing down. He thought, "I'm safe."

About halfway down the vines the man could hear the tiger growling above. But the man also heard an ominous bellowing sound from below. It was a hungry crocodile waiting with its mouth open for a tasty meal when the man reached the bottom. So the man stopped where he was and decided just to wait there until the tiger and crocodile realized their prey had escaped them and would go on their way, and then the man could go on his way. The man had saved himself. But then the man felt the vines shaking and looked up in horror to see two rats, a white rat representing the man's days and a black rat representing his nights, busily chewing the vines.

The man now realized that he had not saved himself and that soon he would either have to climb up and face the tiger or fall down and be eaten by the crocodile. At that point in the story the man sees the Cross of Jesus that provides an escape from the consequences of sin, and the man reached out in faith, grasped the Cross, and was lifted to safety. During the story even some of the adults were tense about how the story was going to turn out. After I finished speaking and was leaving, one of the children came up and said, "Please do not tell that story again. It frightened us." So there are limits that suggest wording the stories we tell for the worldview (which includes the ages) of our listeners.

However, the goal is not to include all the gruesome details but to preserve the intent of the story and, as needed, to speak to the child's worldview understanding and spiritual need. In my own experience in sharing the Bible stories in many rural villages there were many children present who came with their parents and were definitely engaged in listening to the stories. In fact, one of the concerns that I had in the Bible Storying sessions was that the children who heard the stories and were eager to participate in the discussion time would discourage the adults from participating. My teaching was primarily for the adults and I did not want these sessions to turn into a children's story time and so displace the adults. Ideally, it would have been better to have a second person with me to conduct a separate appropriate Bible Storying session for the children. But even that could pose some problem in that the stories the adults heard and the stories the children heard could be different in wording and any alert child would immediately catch that!

Age-graded curriculum guides for preparing lessons for children in the U.S. may be helpful in a general sense to be aware of the development stages of children and what their worldview can process, but not always accurate for children living in many of the less developed nations or rural areas. I will confess that this is not an area of my expertise though I did gain some experience through trial and error while telling and teaching the Bible stories in the Asia-Pacific Region countries where children often joined the teaching since it was the only entertainment in their community.

There is an excellent manual on Bible Storying for children prepared by Kurt Jarvis. Kurt and his wife Judy have some 50 years of experience working with children. Several years ago the Jarvises became aware of the concept of Chronological Bible Storying and coupled this approach with an age-graded curriculum development.[30] They have also included the novel use of a *Storying Quilt* similar to that developed by Carla Clements in her *Visual Story Bible*.[31] The Jarvises are also associated with the International Network of Children's Ministry (INCM) and so are involved in an extensive networking with other children's workers. The Jarvises have considerable experience conducting children's training internationally and gained additional experience from this. Check out both websites for ideas about visualizing Bible stories for children.

As a general rule I found that most of the children in their retelling of the Bible stories tended to use less of the character dialog and retold the stories more as a narrated account of what happened. I realize this is a broad generalization. Some children did preserve quite a bit of the dialog and were able to include it in their stories. Depending on the ages of the children, I would suggest retaining the entire dialog in the simpler stories, and the essential dialog in the longer stories. That is just a rule of thumb.

While I would not want to downplay the presence and effect of sin, I have found that for many of the children that a more positive theme of God's love and provision should receive greater emphasis than the wages of sin. Using *The Flood Story,* again as an example, the major adult themes in the Evangelism Track of stories focus on three themes: 1) the growing evil and wickedness of mankind; 2) God's awareness of the growing sinfulness; and 3) His judgment of it leading to a determination to destroy the evil. Then the focus shifts to finding Noah as a righteous man in his day. So God reveals to Noah what He is about to do and what Noah must do to save his family and the animals. Then as the judgment moves toward destruction the story tells that Noah did all that God commanded him to do. So in Noah's obedience his family and the animals are saved.

For younger children I have often slightly refocused the major story theme to the goodness of God who was pleased with Noah because he was righteous and so God provided a way for Noah and his family and the animals to escape the flood. Then the story moves to the ending as Noah and his family and animals came out of the ark and Noah offered a sacrifice to thank God. So God promised never to destroy the earth by water again and gave the beautiful rainbow as a sign of His promise.

I most likely would not use the story of David and Bathsheba but might use the story of David and Jonathan who were good friends and helped each other. I would use the Joseph story, but would be careful how to word the incident in Potiphar's house with his wife and the false accusation that landed Joseph in prison. The part about Joseph's forgiving his brothers and being reunited would be important.

Most children seem able to handle stories like the plagues in Egypt quite well. Children did well with the story of *The Bronze Serpent* and understood the situation and consequences of disobedience and how obedience helped the people to get well and live.

In terms of worldview I would select and prepare the Bible stories to promote the love and provision of God and how it was important always to obey what God tells us to do or not do. I would not overlook the consequences of sin and the need for repentance and forgiveness. Unless there were other cultural considerations I would include the sacrifices as a way God gave to show repentance and payment for sin. But also that God was preparing a better way in someone He was going to send to help us.

The stories of Jesus are usually not a problem as children quickly see Jesus as a hero who helped people who were afraid, sick or crippled or blind, and even helped dead people come back to life. *The Crucifixion Story* is brutal but most of the Third World children seemed to understand the hate building toward Jesus and that Jesus was taking on himself the punishment for our sin. There was always excitement and joy in *The Resurrection Story*.

89

The story of the *Birth of Jesus* with the *Coming of the Wise Men* with gifts usually catches children's attention. Children like the *Temptation Story* because Jesus did not obey Satan, but did what pleased God instead. The stories of Jesus blessing the children were always attractive as were the "Feeding Stories" as often the children know what it is to go hungry.

In general, I found myself crafting the stories somewhere near the basic crafted story staying close to verbatim that simplified the many details in the stories like numbers and place names, but also that added in proper names and nouns in place of pronouns to make it easy for the children to follow who was speaking to whom. As I mentioned earlier I kept the essential dialog and simplified the longer dialog sequences. So the resulting story was somewhat lightly paraphrased in that it was simplified but no teaching or story expansion was included.

I did not do what many do who tell stories to children. I do not interrupt the stories at various places to ask the listeners: "And what do you think happened next?" I did not use recast stories with children, as I feared their inability to differentiate between what was Bible and what was a recast version.

Following are some illustrations of different story crafting for children using the Adam and Eve story.

> God told Adam, "You can eat fruit from the trees in the garden. But you must not eat any fruit from the tree of good and evil. When you eat fruit from this tree you will surely die."
> God made a wife for Adam so he would not be alone. One day Adam and his wife were in the garden when a clever snake spoke to Adam's wife. The snake asked Adam's wife, "Did God really did say, don't eat any fruit from the trees in the garden?" Adam's wife told the snake they could eat fruit from any tree, but must not eat any fruit from the tree of good and evil in the middle of the garden. The snake told Adam's wife a

lie. He told her that she would not die. The snake made Adam's wife want to eat some fruit from the tree. So she ate some of the fruit and even gave some to Adam and he ate it, too.

Then Adam and his wife knew they disobeyed God. So they became afraid and hid from God. Because they ate the fruit they were ashamed because they were naked. Now they couldn't know God the same way any more. God told Adam that now he must work very hard to grow his food and one day he would grow old and die.

**\*\*\*\*\*\*\*\*\*\***

This paraphrased example is similar to the short (one paragraph) paraphrased Bible stories in the Short Commentary (script) that accompanies the *Look, Listen & Live*[32] color booklets and flipcharts from Global Recordings Network. There is also a set of longer (multi-paragraph) paraphrased story scripts for adults.

The following story is longer with more detail. It would be more appropriate for older children. Notice that the fact of Adam and Eve's nakedness is not included in this story. The focus is on the disobedience as it affects the relationship of Adam and Eve with God.

After God made Adam and Eve they were at peace in their beautiful garden. They did just as God told them to do. They talked with God as someone would talk with their friend, and they did not know of anything evil or wicked. It was important for Adam and Eve to understand that they must always obey God's commands, so God said to Adam and Eve, "You may eat the fruit of all the trees in the garden except one. In the middle of the garden is a tree with fruit on it that you must not eat. If you eat the fruit of that tree, you will certainly die."

Among the animals in the garden there was a clever snake, and this snake said to Eve, "Did God say that you must not eat fruit from *any* tree in the garden?"

91

Eve answered the snake, "We can eat the fruit of all the trees *except* the one that stands in the middle of the garden. If we eat the fruit of that tree or even touch it, God says we will die."

Then the snake said, "No, you will not die. God knows that if you eat the fruit of that tree, you will become as wise as He is, for you will know what is good and what is evil."

Eve listened to the snake, and then she looked at the tree and its fruit. The fruit was beautiful to look at. Eve thought surely it would be delicious to eat. And it would be wonderful to be wise as God. Eve forgot that God had said not to eat the fruit. So she took some of the fruit and ate it, and then she gave some to Adam and he ate it, too.

Immediately Adam and Eve knew they had done wrong by not obeying God's words. Now for the first time they were afraid to meet God when He came to visit. They tried to hide from God's sight among the trees of the garden. When God came to visit He called, "Adam, where are you?"

Adam said, "I heard your voice in the garden, and I was afraid, and I hid myself."

God said, "Why were you afraid to meet me? Have you eaten the fruit from the tree I told you not to eat?"

Adam said, "The woman you made for me gave me some of the fruit and I ate it."

Then God said to the woman, "What have you done?"

Eve said, "The snake told me it would do me no harm, so I took some fruit and ate it."

Then God said to the snake, "Because you caused Adam and Eve to disobey me, you shall no longer walk like other animals. You shall crawl in the dust and the dirt forever. You will hate the woman, and the woman will hate you. You will try to harm her and her children, and they shall try to kill you."

Then God said to the woman, "Because you led your husband to disobey me, you shall suffer and have pain and trouble when you have babies."

And God said to Adam, "Because you listened to your wife and she told you to do what was wrong, you must suffer. You must work for all your food you get from the ground. You will find thorns and thistles and weeds growing from the earth. If you want food, you must dig and plant and reap and work, as long as you live. You came from the ground, for you were made of dust, and your body shall go back into the dust when you die."

Because Adam and Eve had disobeyed the word of God, they had to leave the beautiful Garden of Eden that God had made as their home. To keep Adam and Eve from going back into the garden, God placed his angels before its gate, with swords that flashed like fire.

So Adam and his wife Eve lost their garden, and no man has ever been able to go back to it since then.

\*\*\*\*\*\*\*\*\*\*

The above story is similar to the longer stories in the popular collection of 365 Bible stories edited for older children in the *Bedtime Bible Story Book*.[33] Notice that this example makes more use of dialog in telling the story. The longer story is tailored for reading and not for learning to repeat.

The *Garden of Praise*[34] website also has longer stories for children. Many have found these picture and story-with-lessons resources to be helpful, or suggest how to craft their stories for children. There are also Spanish stories. Stories may be downloaded and used freely but are not to be included in publications for sale.

I realize that in many places where Bible Storying is used there are children present among the adults. The stories are crafted for adult listeners. Children do hear the stories and do understand and remember the stories. But where it is possible to have a separate storying session for children it may be better to have stories prepared especially for them. The choice of stories to tell is probably the main consideration, followed by how the stories are told, and what details are kept or dropped out. Preparing Bible stories for retelling by the children could be an important consideration since this is a helpful activity that encourages participation as well as repetition.

93

# Chapter 9

## Oralizing Stories for Women

As with Bible Storying for children I have also singled out crafting Bible stories for women listeners. This is not to say there is a "man's" way or a "woman's" way, but to point out from personal experience some considerations for paying attention to the specific interests of women listeners and story details that speak to their worldview.

For the most part in the early days of Bible Storying in tribal animistic and later Hindu settings the stories as crafted seemed to work equally well for both men and women. Later when opportunities came for telling the stories among Muslims the original story crafting was doctrinally based primarily for the men. In fact, it was men who gathered to hear the stories and little by little women would come and sit on the perimeter to listen.

The women and children with them would talk quietly among themselves and occasionally stop talking and become intensely interested in the story of the moment. Then they would resume their talking and appear to tune out until another story again caught their interest. It didn't take much observation to notice that it was the stories about women in which women or families were mentioned. Continued observation indicated that great interest was shown related to cultural matters in the stories that related to the women's world.

It took a good bit of worldview exploration to really pinpoint some of the story bits and pieces that caught the women's attention. This was most helpful when later preparing the 90-story resource for women that I titled *God and Woman*. By then, along with those women who were storying among Muslim women, a number of common worldview issues had been identified. These were things in the stories that women found similar to their culture. It included marriage rites, families and family relationships, the meaning of names, barrenness and stories of those who were blessed with children because of some miracle, and many almost insignificant things in the stories that a man motivated to get to the doctrinal minutiae could easily overlook. And sometimes it was a matter of things not mentioned in the stories that left the women wondering.

I'll list a few of these women's interest points that I found in my experience. The women appreciated hearing that God also made woman, even though she was made from bone and flesh of her husband. They saw that God had a purpose in making the first woman and that God gave her and her husband the task of beginning to populate the world. In *The Cain and Abel* story it is the woman who praises God for giving her a son. Later she praises God again when God gives her another son to replace the murdered Abel. The women asked why Noah's wife did not have a name in that story. Abraham's marriage to his half-sister Sarah was not a problem as many among the listeners marry relatives to keep property in the family. They understood the problem with Sarah and her barrenness and of Hagar as a surrogate mother of a son for Sarah. The birth struggles between first wife Leah and loved wife Rachel and their maidservants was of great interest. The meaning of Jacob's children's names was interesting. The women were astounded at the story of Joseph and Potiphar's wife, and that a man could be so pure. I found out later that folk versions of this story were already popular among many of the Muslim women.

Two stories really caught their attention. First was the story *A Bride for Isaac*, the story of Rebekah. The kindness of Rebekah to provide water for Abraham's servant and his camels, the sharing of gold ornaments as gifts for Rebekah, and asking Rebekah if she would go with the servant caught the women's attention. Finally the women listeners responded to that little almost unnoticed event that happened as Rebekah and the servant drew near Isaac who was standing in the field. Rebekah asked who that man was, and the servant replied that it was his master. Then Rebekah drew her veil and covered her face. This said to the women that Rebekah was a modest woman—a good sign. The women liked the story and said it was a good one.

This alerted me to slow down when selecting Bible stories to include in the story sets for Muslim women, and to pay close attention to the small cultural details that it was easy for a man to overlook in crafting the stories while attempting to focus on the spiritual truths. This meant then to include not only more stories about women and their families, but also stories that involved women in some role as the hero, or as one that God helped and blessed in some special way.

Story relationships were very important to include and explore. This posed some concerns about longer stories like that of Ruth and Naomi. But the story crafting needed to preserve all the small details that attracted the women even like Ruth's uncovering Boaz's feet and lying down.

While learning these points of interest I missed several significant details. In preparing the 90-story resource for South Asian Muslim women related to their common worldview issues, I had decided to craft the stories as simple narrated accounts, and to keep only essential character dialog. The reason for this is that so many of the women were nonliterate and even the literate ones had little education. So I assumed that a greatly simplified Bible story was needed. I was wrong and discovered this when field testing the stories. As it turned out there were two problems. One is that the women felt the stories were uninteresting. They wanted to overhear the character dialog and wanted more. So the stories were recrafted to put back all or as much dialog as was practical.

97

In addition the women felt some stories were not interesting because they were not relational enough. So stories were recrafted to add in family names and even to break the chronological guideline of not jumping ahead to pick up some things like the family of Timothy—Lois and Eunice in a story about the Bible. Also a chronological jump was made to bring the story of Hagar forward to an introductory story about *The God Who Sees and Hears*. Listeners were very interested in Abraham's family and relatives. They liked the humor in the stories in Jacob's struggle between Leah and Rachel.

A major flaw in these *God and Woman* stories was not dealing with salvation in a more relational manner that would appeal to the women listeners. Their religion taught that paradise was a destination prepared for faithful men. With a weak understanding regarding sin, living in a culture that did not practice forgiveness, belief in a God that was considered merciful but distant and unapproachable, and an ultimate destination after this life that was not considered desirable, the women were not motivated regarding salvation.

The women were, however, deeply touched by the compassion of Jesus and his attitude toward women in need. So every story and every item in the stories that spoke of God's love, help, blessing, and provision of families was important as they challenged or touched the women's worldview. What was important to them was help in this life. So the women needed to see salvation as a relationship that began in this life with immediate benefit. I had to craft a second set of stories to address the matter of salvation more directly as a relationship with the Father made possible through the Son Jesus. This set with fewer stories and more aggressively evangelistic I called *Heaven is for Women*.

A rural woman stopped me in the story of *The Annunciation* that ended with Mary going to visit her relative Elizabeth. This woman wanted to know how the two women were related, and did not want to continue until she had a satisfactory answer. The answer required quickly reflecting back to Jacob and his sons Levi and Judah and tracing the lineages down through Aaron and David to Elizabeth and Mary. This apparently answered her question and she allowed me to continue.

Another story that caught the women's attention was the story of *The Sinful Woman Who Anointed Jesus.* It has powerful visual details in the woman's touching Jesus' feet with her hair—an act of deep humility and worship. In the South Asian culture the head is holy and the feet are the lowly part of the body. By touching her hair (the head) to Jesus' feet the woman was symbolically bowing before him.

*The Woman With the Issue of Blood* is another powerful image of the impure woman touching Jesus. That story needed a brief introductory story from Leviticus 15 about the consequences of her uncleanness and her resulting plight as a living "dead person" who polluted all that she touched, unable to prepare food for others, to attend the place of worship, and especially to pollute a holy person. She had touched others in the crowd as well and so was fearful of the consequences in being found out. This passage was narrated as a pre-story. I could list many other stories where worldview issues dictated the need for careful crafting for women to maintain interest and relationship with their world.

I suggest that when crafting stories for women listeners, whether a man or woman storyer, that the storyer pay close attention to the small cultural and relational details to preserve that which attracts and holds the interest of women listeners and in doing so, attests that the Bible stories are good stories.

Following are several story examples that illustrate different format options for oralizing Bible stories for women. The first story is a compiled story with a relational connection for the intended listeners. The intent of the story was to introduce in a relational manner the

99

characteristics of God that were critical for those listeners and that would be explored in succeeding stories. Several versions that I have used are *The Living God* for Hindus and *The God Who Sees and Hears* for Muslim women. It is not an exhaustive story on all the moral and spiritual characteristics of God—only an introduction to selected characteristics so that women listeners will be aware of these in the following stories. In the case of Muslim women and the typical worldview that Muslims have about a transcendent God, the story was to introduce a caring God who saw a woman's need and heard her cries—establishing a possible relationship between God and the woman. Note how this story was related specifically to Muslim women:

## The God Who Sees and Hears

The Anointed One who came from God once told a woman that God is a Spirit and all who worship Him must worship in spirit and in truth. One of the prophets declared, "From everlasting to everlasting you are God" (*Ps 90:2b*). Again the prophet said, "....You remain the same, and your years will never end" (*Ps 102:27*).

Long before the earth or heavens were created, or before there were any people on earth, God existed. He has always lived for He had no beginning or end. Because God created everything, He needs nothing from people. All He desires is our true worship and love.

God is loving toward all He has made. God created the first man and first woman and desired to walk and talk with them. God shows His love by providing for all His creation. God makes the sun to shine and the rains to come so our food will grow. God has placed the fish in the rivers and the animals upon the grasslands and mountains for our food. God gives children to families.

God is all-powerful. There is nothing God cannot do. An angel once said, "Is anything too difficult for God?"

God is all knowing. A prophet declared that he could not hide from God. He said that if he went down into the grave, God was even there. If he went up into heaven God was there. Another prophet said that the eyes of God were everywhere keeping watch upon the wicked and the good. God sees and hears everything. Nothing can be hidden from His search and knowledge.

100

A woman named Hagar called God, "the God who sees," because God helped her when no once else saw her need. God also knows what is hidden in your heart; for the prophet also said "God created my inmost being and knit me together in my mother's womb" (Ps 139:13).

Still another prophet declared that God's eyes were too pure to look upon evil. God does not permit anything impure or evil in His presence. All that comes into God's presence must be made clean and pure. And only God can make clean what is unclean. All that is wrong or sinful God will judge. God desires that sinful people confess their sin, turn from their sin and seek His forgiveness and cleansing from sin.

All of these characteristics of God will be more fully revealed in future stories. These stories come from God's Word, the Bible. You will learn to know God better as you listen to the stories and see how God works in the everyday lives of men and women.[35]

**********

Another story from the *God and Woman* stories was included as an affirming story for Muslim women. The story contributes little toward the ultimate goal of leading women to faith in Christ. But the story, by affirming their culture and social expectations does contribute to presenting the Bible stories as *good* stories. This story required some introduction to the Abraham family genealogy that the women enjoyed.

### A Bride for Isaac

Abraham was now very old. God had blessed him in every way. One day Abraham said to his chief servant, "Go to my country and my own relatives and get a wife for Isaac. Make sure that you do not take my son back there, but instead bring the girl here." Then the servant took ten camels loaded with all kinds of good things from Abraham and set out for the place where Abraham's relatives lived. When the servant arrived near that place he made the camels kneel down near a well outside the town, for it was toward evening, the time when women go out to get water.

There the servant began to pray, "O LORD, God of my master Abraham, give me success today. See, I am standing beside this well and the daughters of the townspeople are coming to draw water. May it be that when I say to a girl,

'Please give me a drink,' and she says, 'Drink, and I will water your camels also'—let her be the one you have chosen for Isaac." Before the servant had finished praying, Rebekah came out with her water jar on her shoulder. She was the daughter of Bethuel, the son of Abraham's brother.

The girl was very beautiful and a virgin. She went down to the well and filled her water jar and came up again. The servant hurried to meet her and said, "Please give me a little water from your jar."

"Drink, my lord," Rebekah replied, "and I will draw water for your camels until they have finished drinking." Without saying a word, the servant watched Rebekah fill the water trough again and again until the camels finished drinking. Then the servant took out a gold nose ring and two heavy gold bracelets and gave them to Rebekah.

"Please tell me, whose daughter are you? Is there room in your father's house for us to spend the night?"

"I am the daughter of Bethuel," Rebekah replied. "We have plenty of straw and fodder for the camels, as well as room for you to stay the night." The servant bowed low to the ground and worshiped God. "Praise be to the LORD, the God of my master Abraham, who has given me success." The girl ran to tell her mother's household about these things.

Rebekah had a brother named Laban. When he had seen the gold nose ring and the golden bracelets, Laban hurried out to meet Abraham's servant, and said, "Come, you who are blessed by God. Why are you standing out here? I have prepared a place for you and the camels." Water was brought for the servant to wash his feet and food was set before him. "I will not eat until I have told you why I have come," the servant said.

"Then tell us," Laban replied.

So the servant explained, "My master's wife has borne him a son in her old age, and my master has given him everything he owns. My master made me swear, 'You must not get a wife from among the daughters of the Canaanites in the land where I live, but from among my own people.'"

Then the servant continued, "When I came to the well today I prayed for success. I asked that whoever gave me water and offered to water my camels, that she be the one. Before I finished praying in my heart, Rebekah came out with her water jar on her shoulder. Now, if you will show kindness and faithfulness to my master, tell me; if not, tell me, so I will know which way to turn."

Laban and Bethuel answered, "This is from the LORD; we can say nothing to you one way or the other. Here is Rebekah;

take her and go, and let her become the wife of your master's son, as the LORD has directed." Then the servant brought out the gold and silver jewelry and articles of clothing and gave them to Rebekah. He also gave costly gifts to her brother Laban and her mother. Then the men who were with him ate and drank and spent the night.

When the morning came, the servant said, "Send me on my way to my master."

So the family called Rebekah and asked her, "Will you go with this man?"

"I will go," Rebekah said.

Her family sent her off with their blessing, "May your offspring greatly increase." So Rebekah and her maids got ready and mounted the camels to go with the servant and his men.

When the servant and Rebekah neared the place where Isaac was living, she looked up and saw Isaac coming. "Who is that man in the field coming to meet us?" Rebekah asked.

"He is my master," the servant explained. So Rebekah took her veil and covered herself. The servant told Isaac all that had happened. Isaac brought Rebekah into the tent of his mother Sarah, and he married Rebekah. So she became his wife, and Isaac loved Rebekah and was comforted after his mother's death.[36]

\*\*\*\*\*\*\*\*\*

Another story that has been popular among both Muslim and Hindu women is the story of *The Sinful Woman Who Anointed Jesus*. This story is directly related to the evangelism objective as it deals with repentance and forgiveness and ends by Jesus blessing the woman, an act that is very cultural.

## The Sinful Woman Who Anointed Jesus

It happened that one of the religious leaders named Simon who was a Pharisee invited Jesus to have a meal at his house. So Jesus went to Simon's house and was reclining at the table. (*In those days it was the custom to recline on a couch when eating.*)

A certain woman who had lived a sinful life in that town learned that Jesus was eating at the Pharisee's house. The woman came bringing a sealed jar of expensive fragrant perfume. She stood behind Jesus at his feet weeping and began to wet Jesus' feet with her tears. Then the woman wiped Jesus' feet with her hair, and kissed his feet and poured perfume on Jesus' feet.

When Simon the Pharisee who had invited Jesus saw all this happening, he thought to himself, "If this man were really a prophet, he would know who is touching him, and what kind of a woman she is—that she is a sinner!"

But Jesus knew what Simon was thinking and so answered him, "Simon, I have something to tell you."

"Tell me, teacher," Simon replied.

So Jesus told this story:

There were two men who each borrowed money from a moneylender. One owed the moneylender an amount equal to a year and a half's wages. The other owed about two months' wages. Neither of the men had the money to repay what was owed. So the moneylender cancelled the debts of both men. Now which of the two men will love the moneylender more?

Simon the Pharisee replied to Jesus, "I suppose the one who had the bigger debt cancelled."

"You have judged correctly," Jesus said. Then Jesus turned toward the woman and said to Simon, "Do you see this woman? I came into your house. You did not give me any water for my feet, but she wet my feet with her tears and wiped them with her hair. You did not give me a kiss of greeting, but this woman, from the time I entered, has not stopped kissing my feet. You did not anoint my head with fragrant oil, but this woman poured perfume on my feet. So I tell you, her many sins have been forgiven—for she loved much. But the one who has been forgiven little loves little."

Then Jesus said to the woman, "Your sins are forgiven."

The other guests began to say among themselves, "Who is this who even forgives sins?"

Jesus said to the woman, "Your faith has saved you; go in peace."[37]

✳✳✳✳✳✳✳✳✳

For the women this story and *Jesus Forgives an Adulterous Woman* could be clustered to provide a stronger forgiveness theme. In a similar manner other stories like *The Raising of Jairus' Daughter*, *Jesus Restores a Widow's Only Son to Life*, and *The Raising of*

*Lazarus* could be clustered to give a strong focus on Jesus' authority over death and a strong relationship to issues of life for the women listeners. Incidentally, the preceding stories were not crafted primarily for easy memory and repetition, but for making a strong presentation among those often hostile to an evangelical message.

Other stories are shorter like *Jesus Restores a Widow's Only Son to Life*. This again is a profound story for women because of the cultural view that a woman must have a male protector. The woman was a widow so she had lost her husband and now her only son is dead. Among many women in these cultures a mother is perhaps closer to her oldest son than even to her husband.

## Jesus Restores a Widow's Only Son to Life

Whenever Jesus saw people in great need he stopped to help them. Because of his miracles and teaching many people followed Jesus. A short time before Jesus had healed the servant of a Roman soldier. The Roman soldier had faith in Jesus to heal the servant. The soldier confessed his faith in Jesus. When Jesus heard his words he was amazed and said to the people, "I tell you, I have not found such great faith even among the crowds!"

Soon afterward, Jesus was near a small town. Jesus' disciples and a large crowd of people went along with Jesus listening to Jesus' words as he taught them. Soon Jesus and his followers approached the gate of the town. There was a funeral procession just coming out of the gate headed for the burial ground. The dead person was a young man, the only son of a grieving widow woman who followed along with many mourners weeping and crying out, as was their custom.

When Jesus saw the widow and her sadness and great loss of her only son, his heart went out to her. So Jesus comforted the woman saying, "Don't cry."

Then Jesus went up to the coffin and touched it. The men carrying the coffin stood still. Jesus spoke to the dead man, "Young man, I say to you, get up!" Immediately the dead man sat up and began to talk. Jesus gave the young man back to his surprised mother.

The people were filled with great awe and began to praise God. The people said, "A great prophet has appeared among us. God has come to help His people." So the news about Jesus began to spread throughout the surrounding country.

At another time on a worship day Jesus was teaching in one of the worship halls. A woman was present who was crippled by an evil spirit for eighteen years. The woman was bent over and could not straighten up at all. When Jesus saw the woman, he was filled with compassion and called the woman to come to him. Jesus said to her, "Woman, you are set free from your infirmity."

Then Jesus put his hands on the woman, and immediately she straightened up and began to praise God for His mercy.

Some of the people who saw this were not happy because Jesus had healed on a worship day. The leader of the worship hall rebuked Jesus saying, "You have six days to do healing, but not on the Holy Day."

Jesus answered the leader, "You hypocrite! Don't you even give water to your animals on the Holy Day? Then should not this daughter of Abraham that Satan has kept bound for eighteen long years be set free on the Holy Day from what bound her?"

The people who opposed Jesus were humiliated, but the people who saw what Jesus did for the woman were delighted with all the wonderful things he was doing.[38]

**********

This story as originally prepared had many items in it that I later learned to improve for telling among the intended listeners. One of those was to replace many of the pronouns used in the verbatim story with nouns and proper names. Some of the Jewish terminology was altered since these stories were originally intended for Muslim women. So "synagogue", "Israel", and "Sabbath" were replaced with more neutral terms. The town's name (Nain) was not essential to the storyline. And since the original story was fairly brief, I chose to continue with a second story that also demonstrated Jesus' compassion as well as defense of an unfortunate woman who had suffered a long time.

106

Among *Grief Stories From the Bible* I selected stories in which Bible women suffered some misfortune and then ended each story with how God redeemed the woman's life. This required a bit of creative story titling and a closure statement. The *Flood Story* is titled *Four Women Who Lost Their Families*. It is still the same story but slightly refocused on the four women and their role following the Flood.

Next is the story of Ruth that is a long story that I have telescoped somewhat while still retaining the flow of the original story and the dialog that makes the story so lifelike. I have retained all the names in this particular story and usually suggest a review of the genealogy before or after telling the story. *Grief Stories From the Bible* has a list of names found in the stories and their meaning because the women often ask what names mean. The story was not crafted in view of easy retelling.

## A Young Woman's Only Hope

There was a famine in the land of Judah so Elimelech and his wife Naomi left Bethlehem where they lived and went into the nearby land of Moab with their two sons Mahlon and Kilion. After a time Elimelech, Naomi's husband, died. The two sons each married a Moabite woman, one named Ruth and the other Orpah. After the family had lived there ten years, both Mahlon and Kilion died, leaving Naomi a widow without her husband and without her two sons. Naomi heard God had provided food in her own land, so she and her widowed daughters-in-law prepared to return.

Naomi said to her two daughters-in-law, "Go back, each of you, to your mother's home. May God show kindness to you, as you have shown to your dead husbands and to me. May God grant that each of you will find rest in the home of another husband." Then Naomi kissed them and they wept aloud. The two women said to Naomi, "We will go back with you to your people." But Naomi insisted, "Return home, my daughters. Why would you come with me? Am I going to have any more sons, who could become your husbands? Return home, my daughters, I am too old to have another husband. Even if I had a husband tonight and then gave birth to sons—would you wait until they grow up? Would you remain unmarried for them? No, my daughters. It is more bitter for me than for you, because God's hand has gone out against me."

At this the young women wept again. Then the one named Orpah kissed her mother-in-law good-by, but Ruth clung to Naomi. "Look," said Naomi, "your sister-in-law is going back to her people and her gods. Go back with her."

But Ruth replied, "Don't urge me to leave you or to turn back from you. Where you go I will go, and where you stay I will stay. Your people will be my people and your God my God. Where you die I will die, and there I will be buried. May God deal with me, be it ever so severely, if anything but death separates you and me." When Naomi realized that Ruth was determined to go with her, Naomi stopped urging Ruth to return to her home.

So Naomi and Ruth continued back to Bethlehem. When the two women arrived the whole town was stirred because of them. The women of the town exclaimed, "Can this be Naomi?"

"Don't call me Naomi," she told them. "Call me *Mara* because God has made my life very bitter. I went away full, but God has brought me back empty. Why call me Naomi? God has brought misfortune upon me." Naomi returned with Ruth to Bethlehem at the beginning of the barley harvest.

Naomi had a relative on her husband's side named Boaz, a man of standing. Ruth said to Naomi, "Let me go to the barley fields so that I might pick up the leftover grain wherever I find favor."

Naomi said, "Go ahead, my daughter." Ruth began to glean in the field belonging to Boaz.

When Boaz came to the field he greeted the harvesters and then asked, "Whose young woman is that?"

The foreman replied, "She is from Moab and returned with Naomi. She asked to glean and gather among the sheaves behind the harvesters. She went into the field and has worked steadily until now, except for a short rest."

Boaz said to Ruth, "My daughter, listen to me. Don't go and glean in another field, and don't go away from here. Stay here with my servant girls. I have told the men not to touch you. And whenever you are thirsty, go get a drink from the water jar my men have filled."

When Ruth heard these words, she bowed low to the ground and said, "Why have I found such favor in your eyes that you notice me, a foreigner."

Boaz replied, "I have been told all about you and what you have done for your mother-in-law since the death of your husband—how you left your father and mother and your homeland and came to live with a people you do not know. May you be richly rewarded by the God of Abraham, under whose wings you have come to take refuge." At mealtime Boaz invited Ruth to come and share bread and roasted grain. Ruth ate all she wanted and then got up to begin gleaning again. Boaz told his men to drop some stalks of grain for her. Later Ruth threshed her grain and took the barley back to Naomi.

When Naomi asked where she had gleaned, Ruth told her about Boaz. Then Naomi said, "May God bless him! God has not stopped showing kindness. Boaz is a close relative; he is one of our kinsman-redeemers."

Ruth added, "He said to stay with his workers until they finish harvesting the grain." Ruth gleaned until the end of the barley and wheat harvests. During this time Ruth continued to live with Naomi, her mother-in-law.

One day Naomi said to Ruth, "My daughter, I should try to find you a home where you will be provided for. Tonight Boaz will be winnowing his barley on the threshing floor. So wash and perfume yourself and put on your best clothes. Then go down to the threshing floor, but don't let him know you are there until he has finished eating and drinking. When he lies down, go and uncover his feet and lie down. He will tell you what to do."

"I will do what you say," Ruth replied. So Ruth went down to the threshing floor and did everything Naomi told her to do.

When Boaz finished eating and drinking and lay down in good spirits, Ruth approached quietly and uncovered his feet and lay down. In the middle of the night Boaz woke up and discovered Ruth lying there. "Who are you?" he asked.

"I am your servant Ruth," she replied, "Spread the corner of your garment over me, since you are a kinsman-redeemer."

"God bless you, my daughter, this is a great kindness you have shown me. You have not run after the younger men, whether rich or poor. Don't be afraid. I will do for you all you ask. All the townsmen know that you are a woman of noble character. But there is a kinsman-redeemer who is nearer kin than I. If he wants to redeem, good, if not, I will do it."

Ruth got up before morning and returned to Naomi who asked, "How did it go, my daughter?" Ruth told her everything that happened. Then Naomi said, "Boaz will not rest until the matter is settled today."

Boaz went into the town and approached the nearer kinsman-redeemer and said, "Naomi, who has come back from Moab, is selling the piece of land that belonged to her husband Elimelech. I thought to bring the matter to your attention. Will you redeem it?"

"I will redeem it," the kinsman-redeemer said.

Then Boaz said, "On the day you buy the land from Naomi and from Ruth the Moabitess, you also acquire the dead man's widow to maintain the name of the dead with his property."

Hearing this, the kinsman-redeemer replied, "Then I cannot redeem it as it might endanger my own estate." So the kinsman-redeemer said, "Buy it yourself. I cannot do it." All the town elders sitting at the gate heard the agreement.

So Boaz took Ruth as his wife. Ruth conceived and gave birth to a son. The women said to Naomi, "Praise be to God, who this day has not left you without a kinsman-redeemer. He will sustain you in your old age. For your daughter-in-law who loves you is better than seven sons." Then Naomi took the child, laid him in her lap and cared for him. The women living there said, "Naomi has a son!" He was named Obed. He was the father of Jesse who was the father of King David. God turned Ruth's sadness and Naomi's bitterness into joy. And God had a purpose for the child who was an ancestor of the Promised One of God who would bless all people. [39]

\*\*\*\*\*\*\*\*\*

*Grief Stories From the Bible* were prepared originally for use with Muslim women who were not interested in any "Christian" teaching but who did enjoy stories about women and especially stories of women who suffered misfortunes like they did. So the stories are very relational, touching their worldview, but also containing a subtle thread leading to Jesus and invitation to believe. In actual use the stories provoke discussion and questions— the very thing the women initially said they were not interested in hearing.

# Chapter 10

## Oralizing Bible Stories
## For Ministry

Crafting Bible stories for retention and reproducibility is one of the objectives in preparing stories to tell. In the case of ministry stories, however, the major objective is to touch listeners' hearts to bring a word of encouragement and comfort while planting seeds that ultimately lead toward Jesus and salvation. The previously mentioned *Grief Stories From the Bible* was originally intended to break through the barrier of "Christian" teaching for Muslim women. The stories, because of the misfortune and redemption themes, also lend themselves well to ministry. In fact, these stories are often included among several other story sets primarily intended for disaster response and relief ministry.

These additional sets are *Water Stories from the Bible*, *Hope Stories from the Bible*, and *Food Stories from the Bible*. *Water Stories from the Bible* was adapted first to be used in clean water projects in Cambodia and Bangladesh. The idea was to use the several themes of water found in Bible stories to take advantage of onlooker interest in water projects. Again a subtle evangelistic theme runs through the stories to emerge strongly in the final stories. Forethought regarding these criteria related to ministry use, worldview relationship, and evangelism objective helped to define the story crafting. Following is an early water story and a later story showing the strengthening theme development.

### Change of Heart
### At the Bottom of the Sea

A certain people living in a city called Nineveh were very sinful in the eyes of the LORD. For God's eyes are everywhere keeping watch on both the wicked and the good. So the word of the LORD came to a prophet named Jonah saying: "Go to the great city of Nineveh and preach against it, because its wickedness has come up before me."

But Jonah ran away from the LORD and instead headed for the seaport where he paid the fare and boarded a ship.

While Jonah was fleeing from the LORD, the LORD sent a great wind on the sea and such a violent storm arose that the ship threatened to break up. All the sailors were afraid and each began to cry out to his own god to save him from the storm. The sailors even threw all the cargo into the sea to lighten the ship. Jonah had gone down inside the ship where he lay down and was fast asleep.

The ship's captain awakened Jonah saying, "How can you sleep? Get up and call on your god! Maybe he will take notice of us and we will not perish."

The sailors cast lots to see who was responsible for the storm. The lot fell on Jonah who confessed, "I am running away from my God. I worship the LORD, the God of heaven, who made the sea and the land." Then Jonah added, "If you pick me up and throw me into the sea it will become calm. I know it is my fault this great storm has come upon you."

The sailors did their best to save the ship, but the storm increased its fury. They cried to the LORD, "Do not hold us accountable for killing this man." Then the sailors took Jonah and threw him overboard and the raging sea became calm.

The LORD had prepared a great fish to swallow Jonah. So Jonah was inside the fish three days and three nights. From inside the fish Jonah prayed to the LORD his God. He said:

*In my distress I called on the LORD, and he answered me. I called for help and you listened to my cry. You hurled me into the deep, into the very heart of the sea, and the currents swirled about me, all your waves swept over me.... seaweed was wrapped around my head.... But you brought my life up from the pit. When my life was ebbing away, I remembered you, LORD, and my prayer rose to you in your holy temple. For those who cling to worthless idols forfeit the grace that could be theirs. With a song of thanksgiving I will sacrifice to you and what I have vowed I will make good. Salvation comes from the LORD.*

The LORD commanded the fish and it spit Jonah out onto dry land. Then the word of the LORD came to Jonah a second time saying: "Go to that great city of Nineveh and proclaim to it the message I give you."

Jonah obeyed the word of the LORD and went to Nineveh. Now Nineveh was a very large city so it took three days for Jonah to go all through it proclaiming the LORD's message: "Forty more days and Nineveh will be destroyed."

When the people of Nineveh heard the message they believed God. So the people declared a fast and all of them from the greatest to the least put on sackcloth as a sign of their repentance. Even the king arose from his throne, removed his royal robes, covered himself with sackcloth and sat in the dust. The king issued a decree saying: "Do not let any man or beast, herd or flock, taste anything, do not let them eat or drink. Let all the animals be covered with sackcloth. Let everyone call urgently on the LORD. Let them give up their evil ways and their violence. Perhaps the LORD may relent and with compassion turn from his fierce anger so that we may not perish."

When the LORD saw what the people did and how they turned from their evil ways, the LORD did have compassion on the people of Nineveh and did not bring upon them the destruction He had promised.

Jonah was angry that the LORD had spared the wicked people of Nineveh instead of destroying them. Jonah said that was why he ran away in the ship, because he knew the LORD would be gracious and compassionate, a God slow to anger and abounding in love.

The LORD said to Jonah, "Nineveh has a very great crowd of people who cannot tell their right hand from their left, and many cattle as well. Should I not be concerned about that great city?"[40] [Just a reminder: In some worldviews it would be best not to use "the LORD" but to use "Jehovah" or "LORD Jehovah" as the word "LORD" alone can be misunderstood or applied to some local deity.]

\*\*\*\*\*\*\*\*\*\*

For this next story I am listing the Scripture references to show the components that I assembled into this compiled story. There is a core story of the crucifixion where Jesus' thirst is introduced or framed by other water references leading up to the core story. This story was not intended for teaching to listeners so the story was not formatted for this purpose. *The Water Stories* were prepared for relief ministry purposes to take advantage of gathered onlookers at project sites.

## Jesus Thirsted So That
## We Might Freely Drink

Exo 3:8; Deu 11:14-15; 2Chr 7:13-14; Psa 69:21; Isa 53; Jer 31:9; Mat 27:34; Lk 22:20; Jn 4:14; 6:35; 7:37; 19:28-30, 34

In the stories of God's people in the part of the Bible called the Old Testament, the land that God gave to Abraham and his descendants was called a land "flowing with milk and honey." God promised to provide abundant water in due season so the crops would be plentiful. Because the Israelites were also shepherds, there would be water for their flocks and green grass for the animals. When their King Solomon built the new temple as a place to worship God, he prayed for the nation and its people. Then God appeared to Solomon in a dream and said:

*When I shut up the heavens so that there is no rain, or command the locusts to devour the land or send a plague among my people who are called by my name, if my people, who are called by my name will humble themselves and pray and seek my face and turn from their wicked ways, then will I hear from heaven and will forgive their sin and will heal their land (2 Chr 7:13-14).*

God knew the people would soon forget and would stumble into sin, and God's judgment would swiftly follow. The people did sin, and the people went into exile as their punishment. In due time God brought the people back to the land of promise. Through the prophet Jeremiah God said,

*I will bring them back. They will come with weeping; they will pray as I bring them back. I will lead them beside streams of water on a level path where they will not stumble... (Jer 31:9).*

God had a plan for his Anointed One to come to His people. This Anointed One would be despised and rejected by his own people. He would take upon himself their infirmities and carry their sorrows. He would be stricken by God and his body pierced for their sins and ours, his punishment would bring peace, for by his wounds sinners would be healed.

The Anointed One would be put to death like a criminal and buried among the rich. But his body would not decay in the

114

grave for he would be raised to life again and would return to the Father in heaven. In doing this he would pour out his life unto death, the innocent suffering for the guilty.

A prophet said about God's Anointed One, "They put gall in my food and gave me vinegar for my thirst" (*Psa 69:21*).

On the night before Jesus was crucified he met with his disciples for a special meal. It was the time when the Jewish people remembered how God's angel had spared their lives in Egypt, by passing over their houses marked with the blood of a lamb. As Jesus ate with his disciples he took the cup of drink made from grapes and said to the disciples, "Drink from it, all of you. This is my blood of the covenant, which is poured out for many for the forgiveness of sins" (*Mat 27:27-28*).

Later that night Jesus was arrested and tried, accused of saying he was the Son of God, which he was. For this Jesus was sentenced to death by crucifixion—to be nailed to a wooden cross and hung up to suffer and die of thirst and exhaustion. At the place of execution the soldiers offered Jesus a drink of wine mixed with gall as a drug to deaden the pain. But when Jesus had tasted it, he would not drink it.

After removing Jesus' clothing, soldiers nailed Jesus through his hands and feet to a wooden cross and crucified him between two criminals just like the prophet had said. Jesus prayed for his enemies asking God to forgive them.

Later that day it became very dark and Jesus cried out in a loud voice, "My God, why have you forsaken me?" It was the time when Jesus took upon himself the sins of the people—the innocent suffering for the guilty. God accepted Jesus' sacrifice. After Jesus had cried out, "It is finished!" he said, "I am thirsty."

One of the soldiers who had crucified Jesus put a sponge on a reed and filled it with vinegar and put it to Jesus' lips. When Jesus had tasted from the sponge, he said, "Father, into your hands I give my spirit," and Jesus bowed his head and died. Later a soldier took his spear and pierced the side of Jesus bringing a sudden flow of blood and water from the wound.

During his ministry Jesus told many listeners that he had living water to give. He said, "If a man is thirsty, let him come to me and drink" (*Jn 7:37*). And again Jesus had said to the woman at the well, "Whoever drinks the water I give him will never thirst. The water I give him will become in him a spring of water bubbling up to eternal life" (*Jn 4:14*). And again, "He who believes in me will never be thirsty" (*Jn 6:35b*).

Because of Jesus' thirst on the cross, we may drink deeply and freely of his salvation leading to eternal life. In the old days God had punished His people when they sinned by withholding the rains so the land was dry and the people became thirsty. Now God in his mercy was offering an abundant pardon for sin and an abundant flow of living water for cleansing sin and quenching the thirst of sinners. In these stories that river of life-giving water has flowed your way. It is yours to drink.[41]

∗∗∗∗∗∗∗∗∗∗

Next is an example of a ministry Hope Story. This set of stories is arranged chronologically, but was prepared to be used selectively and independently during disaster response or relief ministry. The initial evangelism theme is again subtle for use among listeners who are possibly hostile but may be more receptive due to the relief work.

## Hope for a Paralyzed Man

It was during feast time that Jesus went to a certain city. Now in that city near one of the city gates there is a pool of water surrounded by five covered porches. Here a great number of disabled people gather and lie there—some who were blind, some lame, and some paralyzed. It was a popular belief that from time to time an angel from God would come and stir the water. Whoever was able to get into the water first would be healed.

A man who had been an invalid for thirty-eight years was there. Jesus saw the man lying on his mat and learned that the man had been in this condition for a long time. So Jesus asked the man, "Do you want to get well?"

The invalid man replied, "Sir, I have no one to help me into the pool when the water is stirred. While I am trying to get in, someone else goes down ahead of me."

Then Jesus said to the man, "Get up! Pick up your mat and walk." At once the man was cured; the man picked up his mat and walked.

When some of the leaders heard about what happened they asked the man, "Who is this fellow who told you to pick up your mat and walk?"

The man who had been healed replied, "It was the man who made me well who told me to pick up my mat and walk." The man who was healed did not know who had healed him because Jesus had slipped away into the crowd of people.

Later Jesus found the man at the place of worship and said to him, "See, you are well. Stop sinning or something worse may happen to you." The man who had been healed went away and told the leaders that it was Jesus who had made him well. That is the story from God's Word.[42]

**\*\*\*\*\*\*\*\*\*\***

This last illustration of a ministry story is from *Food Stories From the Bible*. It represents an enhanced (harmonized) story that is a blending of *Jesus Feeds the Five Thousand* stories found in all four Gospels. Typically it is best to take the longest account as the base and then add details from the other parallel accounts. This principle holds true for parallel accounts of the parables as well. *The Greatest Story,*[43] that is a harmonizing of the four Gospels into one unified set of episodes or stories and each told as a story, illustrates this procedure. The story of the feeding of the 5,000 is told in this book and is perhaps the most popular "food" story in the Bible.

## Food for the Hungry Multitude

Jesus said to his disciples, "Come away with me to a wilderness place and rest for a little while." So Jesus took his disciples by boat to the other side of the lake. But the crowds of people saw Jesus leaving; many recognized him, so the crowds hurried on foot in that direction. They followed Jesus because the crowds saw the miraculous signs when Jesus healed the sick. The people arrived before Jesus and were waiting for him. When Jesus saw the great crowd, he was moved with compassion because the people were like sheep having no shepherd. So Jesus welcomed them and began to teach the people many things. Jesus talked with the people about the Kingdom of God and healed those who needed healing.

Now it was late in the day. Jesus went up on the mountain and sat down with his disciples. The disciples said to Jesus, "This is a remote place, and it's already very late. Send the people away so they can go to the villages and buy something to eat."

Jesus answered the disciples, "You give them something to eat."

"But that would take eight months of a man's wages! Are we to go and spend that much on bread and give it to the people to eat?" the disciples asked.

"How many loaves do you have?" Jesus asked. "Go and see."

When the disciples found out, they said to Jesus, "Five loaves and two fish."

"Bring the food to me," Jesus said, and then asked the disciples to have all the people sit down in groups on the green grass. The people sat in groups of fifty and one hundred.

Jesus took the five loaves and two fish and looked up to heaven. Jesus thanked God for the food and then broke the loaves and gave the pieces to the disciples to give the people. Jesus also took the two fish and in the same manner thanked God and divided the fish for the disciples to give the people.

The people ate the food until satisfied. Afterward Jesus told his disciples to gather up the remaining food so that nothing is lost. The disciples picked up twelve basketfuls of broken pieces of bread and fish left by those who had eaten. Jesus fed the people who were too many to count, a great many men, besides the women and children.[44]

**********

In the same manner other ministry stories can be used verbatim "as is" or crafted by compiling parallel accounts. Essential story details are kept and any details that might be confusing or possibly draw listeners away from the reason for telling the story should be carefully considered whether to include, revise or leave out.

Let me stress that these examples are my versions of crafting or oralizing Bible stories for telling. Each storyer must pray about preparing their stories according to what the storyer is comfortable in doing and according to what is needed for their listeners and their worldview.

# Chapter 11

## Illustration of Basic Story Crafting

Let's look at the process of crafting a story for telling. I have chosen the following story from the life of King Saul as a difficult one because of the details. It is not a commonly used story but it illustrates the process of simplifying a detailed story. We begin with the verbatim story. In your Bible read the verbatim story in 1 Samuel 13:1-14. These verses recount the story of Saul's offering an unauthorized sacrifice. The sacrifice was only to be offered by a priest—a descendant of Aaron or someone consecrated by God like Samuel.

This story is seldom used in an evangelism track, but has value when dealing with obedience in discipling or leader training. I use this story to illustrate a story with content that makes it difficult or confusing to tell to listeners. When you have read the story and are familiar with it and all its details, then read on to see what might need to be done in preparing it as an oral story.

You can see there is quite a bit of detail in the verbatim account. I am going to use strike-through to eliminate some of the detail while keeping as much verbatim wording as possible to simplify the story without changing its storyline while staying close to original wording.

### *Edited Verbatim Story*

Saul was thirty years old when he became king, and he reigned over Israel ~~forty-two years~~. Saul chose three thousand men from Israel; two thousand were with him ~~at Micmash and~~ in the hill country ~~of Bethel~~, and a thousand were with Jonathan ~~at Gibeah in Benjamin.~~ The rest of the men he sent back to their homes.

Jonathan attacked the Philistine outpost ~~at Geba,~~ and the Philistines heard about it. Then Saul had the trumpet blown throughout the land and said, "~~Let the Hebrews~~

119

hear!" ~~So all Israel heard the news:~~ "Saul has attacked the Philistine outpost, and now Israel has become a stench to the Philistines." And the people were summoned to join Saul ~~at Gilgal~~.

The Philistines assembled to fight Israel, with three thousand chariots, ~~six thousand charioteers,~~ and soldiers as numerous as the sand on the seashore. ~~They went up and camped at Micmash, east of Beth Aven.~~

When the men of Israel saw that their situation was critical and that their army was hard pressed, they hid in caves and thickets, among the rocks, and in pits and cisterns. Some ~~Hebrews~~ even crossed the Jordan ~~to the land of Gad and Gilead.~~ Saul remained ~~at Gilgal,~~ and all the troops with him were quaking with fear.

He waited seven days, the time set by Samuel; but Samuel did not come ~~to Gilgal,~~ and Saul's men began to scatter. So he said, "Bring me the burnt offering and the fellowship offerings." And Saul offered up the burnt offering. Just as he finished making the offering, Samuel arrived, and Saul went out to greet him.

"What have you done?" asked Samuel.

Saul replied, "When I saw that the men were scattering, and that you did not come at the set time, and that the Philistines were assembling ~~at Micmash,~~ I thought, 'Now the Philistines will come down against me ~~at Gilgal,~~ and I have not sought the LORD's favor.' So I felt compelled to offer the burnt offering."

You acted foolishly," Samuel said. "You have not kept the command the LORD your God gave you; if you had, he would have established your kingdom over Israel for all time. But now your kingdom will not endure; the LORD has sought out a man after his own heart and appointed him leader of his people, because you have not kept the LORD's command." (*Edited from NIV verbatim account.*)

∗∗∗∗∗∗∗∗∗∗

The strikeouts remove excess detail that most likely would not make sense to listeners. The "Hebrews" was removed because it introduced another term for "men of Israel." Additional edits and small changes would eliminate still more detail like the numbers of men with Saul and Jonathan and replace them with more easily understandable concrete relational comparisons like similes.

Next we begin the task of further simplifying and adapting the story for clarity in telling and understanding by listeners who do not know all the places nor may be capable of understanding the larger numbers mentioned.

### Basic Crafted Story

King Saul's Disobedience
And Rejection as King

Saul was still a young man when he became king, and he ruled over his people a long time. One day King Saul chose a large army of men from Israel. King Saul kept most of them with him in the hill country and the others were with his son Jonathan in a nearby place.

King Saul's son Jonathan attacked the enemy outpost and all the enemy heard about it. Then King Saul had the trumpet blown throughout the land and said, "Let the people hear!" So all Israel heard the news: "King Saul has attacked the enemy outpost, and now Israel has become a stench to the enemy." So the people of Israel were summoned to join King Saul for the battle.

The enemy assembled to fight Israel, with a very large number of chariots and soldiers as numerous as the sand on the seashore. The enemy went up and camped near King Saul and his army.

The men of Israel saw that their situation was critical and that their army was hard pressed. So they hid in caves and thickets, among the rocks, and in pits and cisterns. Some of King Saul's army even crossed the river to a nearby land. But King Saul remained and all the troops with him were quaking with fear.

King Saul waited seven days, the time set by Prophet Samuel. But Prophet Samuel did not come and King Saul's men began to scatter. So King Saul said, "Bring me the burnt offering and the fellowship offerings." Then King Saul offered up the burnt offering. But just as King Saul finished making the offering, Prophet Samuel arrived. King Saul went out to greet him.

"What have you done?" asked Prophet Samuel.

King Saul replied to Prophet Samuel, "I saw that the men were scattering, and that you did not come at the set time, and that the enemy were assembling against me. I thought, 'Now the enemy will come down against me, and I have not sought God's favor.' So I felt compelled to offer the burnt offering."

Prophet Samuel replied to King Saul, "You acted foolishly. You have not kept the command that your God gave you; if you had, God would have established your kingdom over Israel for all time. But now your kingdom will not endure; God has sought out a man after his own heart and appointed him leader of his people, because you have not kept God's command."[45]

**********

After Saul is mentioned as becoming king I then stereotyped his name as "King Saul" and used it consistently. Samuel is "Prophet Samuel." Also I substituted the proper name for pronouns referring to Saul. The Philistines are now "the enemy" to reduce the number of new names. The number of proper names has been reduced to the main characters—King Saul, Prophet Samuel, and the minor character Jonathan. Large numbers are suggested concrete-relationally rather than quantified by large abstract numbers. The "Hebrew" references were changed to keep from introducing a new term for the men of Israel. If use of the word "Israel" or "Israelite" were a problem for certain religious worldviews, then a more generic term like "descendants of Abraham" or even "Hebrews" in place of "Israel" could be substituted in order to keep listeners connected and not reacting to names in the stories that could hinder their hearing the rest of the story. At times we might also want to settle on which name to use for God—God or the LORD. In some settings this could be confusing as two different gods. In other settings the language terminology would probably use one word to cover both names—like "Allah."

Dialog references preceded the dialog quotes saying who was speaking to whom. The intent was to keep as much of the verbatim wording and structure but to simplify the story—making it "oralized" for telling while reducing any factors which would hinder receiving the story as a good story, or that could cause confusion to listeners. Dependent clauses if present in the verbatim can complicate telling a story, especially if working with an interpreter. Simple declarative sentences that imply progression or consequence provide appropriate emphasis and clarity in telling.

In the next chapter you will see a paraphrased version of this same story. Paraphrased stories (or summarized) can be used to bridge between stories we want to use for teaching or to use as introductory stories for a key story to follow. The story of Joseph is a commonly paraphrased story that connects the Patriarch stories with the Exodus stories. When bridging, the story flow is more important than including all the scenes and details of the individual episodes that comprise the longer story.

# Chapter 12

## Other Forms of Stories
## Crafted from the Verbatim Story

Other forms of crafted stories include **Extended Stories, Enhanced (Harmonized) Stories,** and **Clustered Stories**. For the preceding story an extended story might begin with King Saul's anointing, his early days as king, then the story of King Saul's disobedience in offering the sacrifice, the story of failing to destroy the Amalekites, and God's rejecting Saul by giving him an evil spirit to torment him and anointing David as new king. It could also continue to events leading to King Saul's death.

Another story that usually benefits from being extended is that of David's sin with Bathsheba and the death of Uriah the Hittite. A pre-story introducing David's bodyguards and naming Uriah is found in 2 Samuel 23. Follow-through stories are summaries of the deaths of four of David's sons in fulfillment of his self-prophecy after hearing Nathan's story of the two men and the little lamb. Following is what that extended story might be.

### God Judges David's Sin

During King David's early years when he was leading the men of Israel against their enemies, one day King David longed for a drink of water from the well near the gate of his home town Bethlehem. Three of King David's valiant soldiers broke through enemy lines and drew water from the well near the gate of Bethlehem and brought it to King David. But King David refused to drink the water and instead poured it out before the LORD as an offering. "This water represents the blood of my men who went at risk of their lives," King David said. His valiant soldiers did many other heroic deeds. King David was very close to these valiant soldiers who protected King David and fought together in King David's army. Among the thirty-seven valiant soldiers were one named Eliam (also called Ammiel) the father of Bathsheba and Uriah the Hittite who was the husband of Bathsheba. (2 Sam 23:13-17, 34, 39)

But one time when King David's army was out fighting the enemy, King David had remained in Jerusalem at his palace. One evening King David could not sleep, so he got up from his bed and walked around on the roof of the palace. King David happened to see a very beautiful woman who was bathing to purify herself from her uncleanness. King David asked his servant to go see who the woman was. The servant reported to King David that the woman was Bathsheba the daughter of Eliam and the wife of Uriah the Hittite, two of King David's valiant soldiers. Then King David sent for Bathsheba and the servants brought Bathsheba to King David. Bathsheba could not refuse the king. So Bathsheba came to King David and he slept with her. Then Bathsheba went back home. Later Bathsheba sent word to King David that she was with child.

So King David sent word to his commander of the army to send Uriah the Hittite back from the fighting. When Uriah the Hittite came, King David asked how the fighting was going and about the commander of the army. Then King David said to Uriah the Hittite, "Go down to your house and spend time with your wife." King David even gave Uriah the Hittite a gift for his wife Bathsheba. But Uriah the Hittite instead slept at the entrance to the palace with King David's servants.

When King David learned that Uriah the Hittite did not go to his own house to his wife Bathsheba, King David asked Uriah the Hittite, "Why didn't you go home?"

Uriah the Hittite replied, "How can I eat and drink in my house and sleep with my wife when the other soldiers are sleeping in tents and fighting the enemy?" Again King David tried to get Uriah the Hittite to go to his wife, but Uriah the Hittite would not. So King David decided to send Uriah the Hittite back to the fighting, and to send a message for the commander of the army to read.

The commander of the army was to put Uriah the Hittite in the front of the fighting and then pull back so that Uriah the Hittite was certain to be killed. When it happened, the commander of the army sent word to King David that Uriah the Hittite was now dead. King David said, "Well the sword devours first one and then another, just continue the fighting."

After Bathsheba mourned for her dead husband Uriah the Hittite, King David sent for Bathsheba and had her brought to the palace as King David's wife. Later Bathsheba bore King David a son. But the thing King David had done displeased the LORD. The LORD sent Prophet Nathan to King David. Prophet Nathan told a story about a rich man who had many sheep and cattle. A poor man had only one sheep that was the family pet.

126

The rich man took away the poor man's sheep and prepared the sheep to feed a friend. When King David heard the story he was furious. "That man must repay four times!" King David demanded.

But Prophet Nathan said, "You are the man!" So Prophet Nathan reminded King David of the terrible wrong he had done in taking another man's wife and causing the unjust death of her husband.

The LORD judged King David's sin and asked, "Why did you despise the word of the LORD by doing what is evil in the LORD's eyes? Now the sword will never depart your house! Out of your own household I am going to bring disaster upon you."

Then King David cried, "I have sinned against the LORD." Prophet Nathan replied, "The LORD has taken away your sin. You are not going to die. But your child with Bathsheba will die." Not long after Bathsheba's baby was born, it became sick and died. Later three more of King David's other sons died violently. One raped his half-sister and her brother killed that son. Then the one who killed his brother rebelled against King David and the army killed him. And finally the oldest surviving son was killed when he desired to take the kingdom for himself.

So King David's judgment against himself was fulfilled. It had happened just as Prophet Nathan warned. King David confessed his sin before the LORD and asked the LORD to create in him a pure heart and to restore the joy of his salvation. The LORD was pleased to do this for King David. Then the LORD gave King David and Bathsheba other sons. God had a special work for one of the sons of King David and Bathsheba to follow David as the new king.[46]

*********

The first part of the story develops David's relationship to Bathsheba's husband and her father as both were among David's bodyguards. The following stories after the main story bring closure or consequences to the main story, thus reinforcing the seriousness of sin in the loss of the love child, David's firstborn son, his beloved son and his oldest surviving son. Early use of only the main story did not make the point of the seriousness of David's sin and the consequences of David's sin. Listeners made allowance for David since he was king. But the entry story provided a new perspective of betrayal and murder. The entire story revealed the consequences of his sin even though God forgave David.

Other stories that benefit from being extended are *The Birth of Jesus* beginning with the *Annunciation* and Joseph's dream, the birth in Bethlehem, the visit of the shepherds and Wise Men, the flight to Egypt, the visit to the temple for Mary's sacrifice, and testimonies of Simeon and Anna. Another story, *The Passion Story,* benefits from being extended beginning with the Last Supper up to the Ascension.

Biographical stories like Jacob, Joseph, and Moses also can be extended. In the New Testament, *The Raising of Lazarus* with introductory story of Jesus' visit in the home of Mary and Martha to establish relationship, the Lazarus story, and followed by the John 12 story of Jesus in the Bethany home of Simon the leper where Mary anoints Jesus. Simon Peter's story may be compiled into an extended story from the references to Peter in the Gospels and Epistles.

Example of an **Enhanced Story (which also can be an Extended Story)** is illustrated by Hezekiah's story with component parts in Kings, Chronicles, and Isaiah, with the core of the story taken from Chronicles and enhanced or added to by the Kings and Isaiah references.

The **Enhanced-only story** is one like *The Feeding of the Multitude* in the chapter on Oralizing Bible Stories for Ministry where there is only one event that is expanded by additional details from parallel accounts. These are not mutually exclusive categories but express the general characteristics of the story format.

In addition to the book *The Greatest Story* (see endnote reference 41) that harmonized the Gospel stories, a paperback chronological narrative account of the Bible story, *The Story from the Book* (see endnote reference 19) is a valuable aid in formatting many of the stories from not only the four Gospels, but also those of the Kingdoms and Prophets, and of Acts and the Epistles. Many times when trying to decide how to prepare a story I have found these two books helpful, especially for the enhanced story formatting.

**Clustered Stories** are those told in groups that center around a common relational theme. The chief value of the clusters is to emphasize or stress a particular truth or theme and occasionally to characterize or contrast Bible characters. Stories may or may not be linked chronologically or related as to cause and effect.

The miracle stories of Jesus are primarily used to characterize Jesus as one having authority over illnesses, disabilities, evil spirits, nature, and even death. By grouping the stories with a similar theme there is a stronger emphasis on the characteristic. Usually three stories are enough for this emphasis.

Many of the teaching parables of Jesus are also presented in clusters, typically in threes. A popular cluster in the Gospels is the cluster of *The Lost Sheep*, *The Lost Coin* and *The Lost Son*.

In the Old Testament there can be cluster stories about leaders both good and bad, disobedience stories, worship stories, sacrifice stories, prayer stories, judgment stories and the like. When story clusters are used and some of the stories are longer, it is best to summarize these longer stories so that a balance exists and the cluster theme is not overwhelmed with details of one much longer story and several much briefer stories.

This next formatting category is one that I had to struggle with. What to do when certain stories were needed but were not found intact in any given place in the Bible? Could the component pieces be pulled together into a coherent narrative? Would such editing compromise the Bible?

## Crafted Compiled Stories
## (based on verbatim components
## and extra-biblical information)

This is a special form of crafted story that cannot be found intact in scripture as verbatim stories, though all the content comes from various scattered verbatim scripture passages except for the story about the Bible which needs some extra-biblical content. These scattered references then imply a narrative that could be assembled into a coherent story. The intent was primarily to provide needed evangelistic or discipling teaching in a narrative format rather than to present an oral Bible. In order to clearly show the various sources of the stories it can be helpful to read these from the Bible first and then say: "Now let me tell this as a story."

There are several commonly compiled stories that I have found useful. One is *The Story of the Bible* to introduce what the Bible is, how it came to be, and what it has to say about itself. Obviously there is some extra-biblical material needed to tell about the 40 or so writers and that the Bible has been translated into many languages. Here is a version done for Muslim women. Note how the story is made relational for the women:

### God's Precious Word

A long time ago a wise teacher named Paul wrote a letter to a young man named Timothy who was just beginning his life's work. Paul wrote to encourage Timothy, because Paul remembered the sincere faith of young Timothy. He said that it was like the faith of Timothy's mother Eunice and his grandmother Lois. Mother Eunice and grandmother Lois each had a strong faith in God. Where did their faith come from? It came from God's Word, Paul said to Timothy,

*Continue in what you have learned and believe is true. Since an infant you have known the holy Scriptures which made you wise about salvation through faith in the One sent from God (2Tim 3:14-15). (Don't*

130

*mention Jesus by name, as there is not yet a story about who he was.)*

Paul reminded Timothy that all Scripture is God-breathed. This means that God caused it to be written. This same Scripture is useful for teaching, training, and correcting so that a person can live a life pleasing to God. Another writer wrote these words, "I have hidden God's Word in my heart so that I might not sin against (*offend*) God." And again he wrote, "God's Word is like a lamp for my feet and a light for my pathway." It shows the correct way to live so that your life would always please God.

Paul wrote other letters to his friends and said that everything written in the past, that is, in God's Word, was written to teach us so that we might have hope. (Rom 15:4) And he said that things about the past were written down as warnings for us in our time. (1 Cor 10:11).

Who wrote down these things? God revealed to many people what they were to write. Sometimes God spoke the words to be written. At other times God's Spirit simply caused the men to faithfully record what happened. Many of these men were called prophets. They lived a long time ago. From the time the first one wrote until the last one was more than 30 lifetimes! (*Moses to John*) Yet there was agreement in what they wrote because God guided their writing.

God's message was to the people who lived in those days, but also to us today. For God's Word is eternal. His message is for all people. Neither the words nor the message will ever pass away. God's Word is like a sharp sword. It is able to penetrate our very souls to judge the thoughts and attitudes of our hearts. It is very powerful.

These words were first written in the language of the people living in that day. God is causing His Word to be translated into all the languages of the world. God wants all people to know the truth about Him and what He has done for us. Today we know these writings as the "Bible" which means "book." There are many writings in the Bible with names like "the Beginning," the "Exodus," the "Judges," and even some named after the prophets who wrote them. You have heard about the *Taurat* and the *Injil* that are parts of the Bible. God has given His Spirit to help us understand the Bible. For God wants us to live by His Word.

\*\*\*\*\*\*\*\*\*

A third commonly compiled story is *The Creation of the Spirit World*. This story has helped in many places to show that God is righteous, creating only good and not evil, and that God is sovereign over even the unseen spirit world, some of which became evil of their own choice and most that continue to serve God faithfully—introducing angels as God's messengers and the evil spirits that test people. Here are the source references for the story components followed by one typical version of that story: Psa 148:2, 5; Col 1:16; Psa 103:20; Heb 1:7 (Psa 104:4); Job 38:7; Eze 28:12b-17a; Isa 14:12-14; Jude 6 (2Pe 2:4); Rev 20:10 (12:7-12); Mat 13:39; Luk 1:19; 24:4; Acts 12:7-10; 1Co 5:5 (1Tim 1:20); Heb 12:22 (Rev 5:11). I did not use every word from each reference. At the time I did this I typed out the references on cards and arranged them in order and then retyped them into the computer and smoothed the story out using paraphrasing if needed.

## God Created the Spirit World

Long ago before God created this world in which we live, or even the first man or woman, God created all the spirits. Because God is righteous (*good, without sin*) He created all the spirits like Himself, for God, too, is a spirit. God has always lived. God is eternal, without beginning or end. In the beginning God commanded and all the spirits were created. They are so many no one can count them. God created the spirits to worship Him and to do the work God gave them. Later God would use the spirits as messengers when God needed to speak to people, to help people, or even to punish people when they sinned against God.

One spirit God created very wise, very powerful, and very beautiful. God had a special work for him to do, to guard God's holy throne in heaven. But this spirit soon was filled with pride because of his great beauty. He said, "I will rule over the other spirits, I will sit in God's place in heaven, I will make myself like the Most High." So this spirit led a rebellion among the other spirits. Because of the spirits' wickedness and rebellion, which was sin against God, the evil spirits were defeated and driven from heaven. Because God is righteous, that is, without sin, He judged the evil spirits' sin and is preparing a special place of eternal punishment for all the disobedient spirits. The powerful spirit who rebelled against God we know today as Satan. His name means *adversary*.

God's Word tells us that Satan is a deceiver, a liar and the father of lies, and a murderer. He seeks to destroy all the good work of God, and especially to tempt people to sin against God. But God is more powerful and is able to overcome the evil work of Satan so that good results, instead of evil. Satan knows that he has been defeated and that his time is short, so Satan is filled with hatred and works furiously against men and women. The other wicked spirits we know as demons or evil spirits. In the coming stories we will see that these spirits feared the One sent from God, for they knew who he was and that he had authority over them.

Most of the spirits remained loyal and obedient to God who created them. God uses these spirits as His messengers to warn against sin, to bring words of judgment whenever people sinned, and to being good news. We know these spirits as angels. Sometimes angels appeared as young men dressed in brilliant white clothing with a golden belt. Sometimes angels appeared as servants of fire. Angels are very powerful and wise. But we are not to worship them, for God created them to serve the people who obey God.

Because God created all the spirits, they were created good like God. When they sinned, God judged their sin, punishing them. God the Creator rules the Spirit World.[47]

**\*\*\*\*\*\*\*\*\***

A fourth commonly compiled story is that of the *Prophet's Message of the Messiah*. The first prophet stories are the popular ones (like Elijah in Sacrifice on Mt. Carmel and Jonah preaching against Nineveh) in which God speaks and acts through the prophets to turn the people back to Him. In other accounts of the message of the Prophets, God begins to speak through these preachers telling of the characteristics, work, and fate of the coming Messiah. Prophecies pointing to the story of Christ can be compiled from numerous passages in the Bible. There are many prophecies and so it is necessary to be selective in choosing the ones that best suit the story strategy. The purpose is to give a preview of Jesus' coming and to provide a transition from the Old Testament stories to the Gospel stories.

133

# The Promised One

One of the men God used to write the Bible said: "In the past God spoke to our forefathers through the prophets many times and in various ways. Some of the prophets that God used were named Moses, David, Isaiah, and Micah. Each prophet told about the coming Messiah or Promised One. God spoke the very first words about the Promised One when He judged the serpent in the days of Adam and Eve. God said that one day the offspring or child of woman would crush the head of the serpent. God later promised Abraham and his son Isaac and his grandson Jacob saying: "Through your descendant all nations on earth will be blessed."

Years later God said through Moses: "The Lord your God will raise up a prophet like Moses from among the people." In the days of King David, God had said: "I will raise up your descendant and will establish the throne of his kingdom forever. I will be his father and he will be my son." The coming Promised One would be born of a virgin in the town of Bethlehem, the home of David. He would be called Mighty God and Prince of Peace. He will rule on the throne of King David. God's spirit would rest upon him. He would be for the honor of Abraham's descendants and a light for all peoples. But he would be rejected by his own people, even though he would heal their sickness and carry their sorrows. He would be betrayed by a friend that shared his bread. He would be falsely accused as a sinner. His hands, feet, and side would be pierced, he would be spit upon and his beard pulled out, yet he would remain silent before his accusers. The sins of all people he would take upon himself though he was innocent of any sin. And he would die among criminals and be buried among the wealthy. But he would live again and return to the Father in heaven.

Before all this happens God would send a mighty prophet like the Prophet Elijah to prepare the way. After these words were spoken many years passed while faithful people trusted God's words and waited for God to fulfill His promises. In a coming story we will learn who that prophet is. [48]

\*\*\*\*\*\*\*\*\*\*

## *Lightly Paraphrased Story*

Now we will review two examples of paraphrasing. The first is a typical simplifying of the story.

## When King Saul Disobeyed God

When Saul became of age he was crowned king of his people Israel. He ruled over his people a long time. During those days an enemy people also occupied King Saul's land. So King Saul chose a large army from among his people. King Saul gave some army to his son Jonathan.

One day King Saul's son Jonathan attacked an enemy outpost and the rest of the enemy heard about it and began to assemble to fight King Saul's army. Then King Saul summoned his people to join him for the battle.

The enemy assembled to fight against King Saul's people with a very large number of chariots and soldiers as numerous as the sand on the seashore. The enemy camped near King Saul and his army.

When King Saul's soldiers saw that they were outnumbered, they became afraid and began to run away and hide in caves and the forest. The soldiers even hid among rocks, and in some holes in the ground and water tanks. Some of King Saul's army crossed the river and fled to a nearby land. But King Saul remained and the soldiers with him were quaking with fear.

King Saul waited seven days for Prophet Samuel to come and offer sacrifices for God's blessing in fighting. When Prophet Samuel did not come, King Saul's men began to run away. Then King Saul offered the sacrifices himself. But just as King Saul finished making the sacrifice, Prophet Samuel arrived, and King Saul went out to greet him.

Prophet Samuel was not pleased that King Saul had offered the sacrifice himself. Then King Saul told the Prophet Samuel that the soldiers were running away. Prophet Samuel did not come at the set time. The enemy was gathering against King Saul and his men. So King Saul thought to himself, "Now the enemy is coming down to attack me, and I have not asked for God's help. Because of this I decided to offer the sacrifice."

Prophet Samuel spoke sharply to King Saul, "You acted foolishly. You have not kept the command the LORD your God gave you. If you had obeyed God, then God would make your kingdom strong and it would last a long time." Also Prophet Samuel said to King Saul, "Your kingdom will not last because you disobeyed God. Now God has chosen another man who is like God's own heart. This man God is anointing to be the new leader. This is happening because you have not kept God's command."

\*\*\*\*\*\*\*\*\*

I have done the light paraphrasing in order to make use of this same story about Saul. I have followed typical practice of paraphrasing to keep the general flow of the story but to make some changes here and there that may make the story easier to follow and clearer to the listener who hears it only once. We might call this paraphrase a "simplifying paraphrase that had no added comment or teaching." What follows next is a deeply paraphrased version of the same story in which additional comment is inserted as part of the story.

### Deeply Paraphrased Story

Now we are going to learn about how King Saul disobeyed God and what God said to King Saul. When Saul became king he was still a young man. He ruled over the people of Israel as their first king for a long time. You remember that the descendants of Abraham were called Israelites after they left Egypt in the days of Moses. And they wanted a king like all the other peoples.

A neighboring enemy people called Philistines occupied part of the land of Israel. They did not like the Israelites and were often fighting them. So King Saul chose a large army from among his people and kept part of the large army with him and gave some of the soldiers to his son Jonathan who commanded his own army. There were some soldiers who came, but King Saul sent them back home because he did not need them right then.

One day King Saul's son Jonathan decided to attack the Philistine enemy at their outpost camp. When word of this reached the rest of the Philistines, they decided to attack the army of King Saul. So the Philistines began to gather in large numbers for an attack. When King Saul saw what was about to happen, he had a soldier blow the trumpet to call more of the men of Israel out to fight.

King Saul had the words sounded to the people: "Listen to the news of what is about to happen! King Saul has attacked the enemy outpost and now the people of Israel have become like a bad smell to the enemy." It wasn't really King Saul who attacked the enemy outpost, but his son Jonathan. The people listened to the news and came to join King Saul in the battle against their enemy the Philistines.

But the Philistine army was very great. There were thousands of chariots and chariot drivers and soldiers as numerous as the sands along the seashore. King Saul was afraid because his army was greatly outnumbered. King Saul forgot to trust in God even after God's Spirit came upon King Saul when he was anointed king. God had spoken to King Saul through the Prophet Samuel saying, "Do whatever your hand finds to do, because God is with you." Also King Saul forgot to tell his men that they, too, should be brave because God was on their side.

Instead, when King Saul's army saw all the Philistines and how many there were, they became really afraid, and began to run away and hide in caves and even down in pits in the ground, and places where water was stored. Some crossed the river into another part of the country. King Saul stayed in that place where he was camped. But all his soldiers were quaking with fear about being outnumbered by the enemy Philistines.

Back in the days of Moses, God told the Israelites how to offer sacrifices that would be pleasing to God. But only a priest was to offer the sacrifice. In fact, some people even died when they disobeyed God's rules about worship. King Saul had waited seven days for the Prophet Samuel to come and offer the sacrifices. But the Prophet Samuel did not come. King Saul wanted God to help him because the enemy was coming in great numbers. King Saul's soldiers were running away, so King Saul decided to offer the sacrifice and victory offering himself.

Then the Prophet Samuel came and asked King Saul what he had done. Prophet Samuel told King Saul that he had acted very foolishly by offering the sacrifice himself. Prophet Samuel knew that God would be displeased because King Saul had disobeyed God's command. So Prophet Samuel told King Saul that he had disobeyed God and, because of this, his kingdom would not last very long. God did not want a king who disobeys Him to rule over the people. Then Prophet Samuel told King Saul that God had chosen another man to be the new king. He was a man who was like God's own heart. All of this happened because King Saul became fearful and acted foolishly when he did not obey God's command.

*********

Obviously I have distorted the story just a bit by inserting teaching comments which are typical of those added by paraphrasers who want to be sure that the listeners "get the point" while the story is being told. In

137

extreme deep paraphrasing even the order of the plot might be rearranged, or even the story paused while lengthy comments were inserted to teach at some point of major interest or emphasis. We might call this paraphrase a "teaching paraphrase."

## Summarized Linking or Bridging Stories

One special form of paraphrased story is the summarized story used for linking or bridging between stories that are major components of your teaching strategy. Bridging stories prevent gaps from occurring in the running stories and serve to connect earlier stories to those that follow. A commonly summarized story is that of Joseph that you realize is actually a long narrative composed of many episodes or events. The purpose in summarizing the story of Joseph is to get the descendants of Abraham into Egypt where the story continues with the slavery, plagues, Passover, and exodus without losing the momentum of the greater Redemption Story at this time. The full story of Joseph is however an excellent story set for later character study and discipling.

### Abraham's Descendants
### Go to Live in Egypt

In a dream God told Abraham that one day his descendants would go to live in a land not their own. This began to happen during the days of grandson Jacob when his son Joseph was sold by his jealous brothers and taken to Egypt as a servant. While working there Joseph was falsely accused of wrongdoing and put into prison for many years. One day the king of Egypt had a dream that no one could interpret. But God helped Joseph to interpret the dream about a coming famine. The king put Joseph in charge of gathering food for the famine. One day during the famine Joseph's brothers came to buy food. They did not recognize Joseph who told them they must bring Joseph's younger brother with them next time. When the brothers came again to buy food and brought Joseph's younger brother, Joseph told his brothers who he was. The brothers were afraid, but Joseph forgave them. Joseph told his brothers to go get his father Jacob and the brothers' families and come live in Egypt. God blessed the family of Jacob and all his sons so that they became a great nation. But God had also said to Abraham that his descendants would be mistreated as slaves. God would punish the people of that country and Abraham's descendants would come out with great possessions.

**\*\*\*\*\*\*\*\*\*\***

Another example of a background story that may be summarized is that of *The Resettlement of Samaria* in 2 Kings 17:24ff that provides a background for *The Parable Good of the Good Samaritan* or *Jesus and the Samaritan Woman* story. We are not interested in all the details of the defeat, exile, and resettlement of Samaria, but there are items in the story that may help to explain why the Jews of Jesus' day disliked the Samaritans. So be sure to look for details that will provide the needed background or reasons for things that happened in the later stories. Summarized bridging/linking stories are usually narrated without the dialog that energizes the major stories.

## The Resettlement of Samaria

The Israelites living in Samaria had continued to sin against the LORD God. So the LORD God caused the Israelites to be defeated by a foreign king who brought in peoples from other countries to take over the towns and settle there. The new people did not worship the LORD God, so the LORD God sent wild animals to kill some of the people. Then the foreign king had some Israelite priests brought in to teach the people how to worship the LORD God. But each group of people made their own gods in the towns where they lived and began to worship these, too. So the people worshiped the LORD God, but they also served their own gods according to the customs of their people. In the following years the people continued this practice of worshiping their own gods. The people were now a mixed people for they had intermarried with the Israelites who still lived in Samaria. Later those Israelites who were pure, that is, had not intermarried with foreigners, disliked the Samaritan people and would not even drink water offered by a Samaritan.

**\*\*\*\*\*\*\*\*\*\***

Notice that I used "the LORD God" to distinguish clearly between "God" and the people's "gods." And I took the liberty of reaching down to the Samaritan Woman story to pick up how the Jews despised the Samaritans. Rather than use this bridging story, one could simply explain from the 2 Kings 17 passage about the Samaritan people and why the Israelites or Jews might despise them in Jesus' day.

Following is a very brief bridging story as an example of condensing the longer King Saul story into a narrative with only minimum details that still captures the essence of the event. This approach employs light paraphrasing because no details from other stories or comments are added to the story. Bridging stories can be most helpful in communicating biblical truth to listeners

### God Rejects Saul as King

In the early days of King Saul's rule his son Jonathan attacked an enemy outpost. This caused the enemy to begin assembling to attack. King Saul sent word for his people to send more soldiers. But the number of enemy was greater than King Saul's army. So King Saul's army began to hide and run away. King Saul was waiting for the Prophet Samuel to come and offer a sacrifice to God. But when Prophet Samuel did not come at the appointed time, King Saul instead offered the sacrifice. Then Prophet Samuel arrived and asked what King Saul had done. Prophet Samuel said; "You have acted foolishly by disobeying God. Now your kingdom will not last. God will seek another king, a man after God's own heart."

**\*\*\*\*\*\*\*\*\*\***

### *Dramatized Story*

Following is an example of a dramatized story and some considerations that affect how it is crafted for performing. There are some other options for dramatizing a story that follows this illustration. The number of readers (actors) needed depends upon the number of characters plus the narrator for telling the story.

## Peter and John Heal a Crippled Beggar
### Acts 3:1-10

*Narrator:* One day the disciples Peter and John were going to the temple. It was time for the mid-afternoon prayer. That day a man who had been crippled from birth was being carried to the temple to beg.

*Crippled man to friends:* Yes, I want you to put me at the same place. Put me in the gate called Beautiful. Begging is good there. Many wealthy people who are able to walk pass that way going to the Temple courts to worship God. They look at me like I did something bad to deserve being cripple. Easy now!

*Friends:* There you are! We'll come get you later. We hope you have good luck with your begging today. Now don't leave without us! Ha! Ha!

*Narrator:* As Peter and John, disciples of Jesus, approach the Temple and are about to enter; the crippled man sees them and persistently begins his begging.

*Crippled man:* Alms! Give me alms! Alms!

*John:* Here is that beggar again! It is bad enough that he sits here to remind us of his pitiful condition. He is always disturbing our worship with his begging. And further, he is blocking our way. Listen, there he goes again, always begging!

*Crippled man:* Alms! Give me alms! Alms! Give me alms! Do you have any money for me?

*Narrator:* Peter and John both stopped before the man who became very excited, thinking he was going to get money from not one but from two people.

*John:* Peter, what should we do? Does this man need money, or do you think forgiveness of sins so God will have mercy on him? The man surely expects something from us.

141

*Peter:* Man, look at us! Silver or gold I do not have, but what I have, I give you.

*Narrator:* The crippled man was giving Peter the older man his full attention. At the mention of silver or gold the man's eyes brightened as he eagerly reached for the alms. Then at Peter's words about not having any, the man fell back disappointed, wondering what Peter meant by his words.

*Peter:* In the name of Jesus Christ of Nazareth, I command you to WALK!

*Narrator:* So Peter reached down and took the crippled man by the right hand and helped the man up. Instantly the crippled man's feet and ankles became strong. The man jumped to his feet and began to walk.

*Crippled man:* I can walk! Praise God! I can walk! Look at me! I can walk!

*Narrator:* And so the man who had been crippled all his former life followed Peter and John into the Temple courts walking and jumping and loudly praising God. When some of the worshipers saw the man, they recognized him as the same crippled beggar that often sat at the gate called Beautiful. The people were filled with amazement, wondering what had happened to the man. The man now held on to Peter and John as more people ran to the Temple court and a crowd began to gather. Peter began speaking to the crowd.

*Peter:* Men of Israel, why does this surprise you? Why do you stare at us as if by our own power or godliness we had made this man walk? The God of Abraham, Isaac and Jacob, the God of our fathers, has glorified his servant Jesus...By faith in the name of Jesus, this man you see was made strong. It is Jesus' name and the faith that comes through Jesus that has given complete healing to this man, as you can all see.

*Narrator:* While Peter was still speaking to the gathered crowd some of the religious leaders and captain of the Temple guard came up to Peter and John and seized them and put them in prison. But many of those present in the crowd who heard Peter's words believed on Jesus and the number of men following Jesus increased greatly that day.

\*\*\*\*\*\*\*\*\*

A drama needs dialog between the characters that tells what is happening or about to happen. The plot is carried by the spoken dialog and the visualized action of the characters and connected if necessary by a narrator. Usually every character in a story will have something to say. In the story of Peter and John healing the lame man at the Temple gate in Acts 3, only Peter speaks in the Bible account. For good drama the lame man and John also need to speak. Drama works best where there is confrontation or discussion between characters and not just narrated action. As the act of begging is visualized and perhaps first John's and then Peter's reaction to the beggar is spoken and enacted, the drama comes to life.

So the story is expanded by the added dialog that is assumed, but is not necessarily scriptural. It is quite possible for additional and even unwanted elements to be inserted into the storyline by both the dialog and by the actions of the characters. Once I was watching a group of Kui tribals act out the *Parable of the Prodigal Son*. It was going okay until the scene with the pigs. The action of the pigs caused the listeners to begin laughing and I feared the actors were making a mockery of the story. Just as I was despairing, the old father appeared and the son rose to go meet him. It was a touching scene as the son fell at the father's feet. Then I realized that the laughter of a few moments before the reconciliation scene had now changed to tears as the listeners were moved by the son's humble return and the father's forgiving love. So I guess that you win some and lose some and pray that the stories, however enacted, will touch hearts.

Many stories leave much to be interpreted by the actors. In *The Good Samaritan Story* the actions of the robbers, the priest and the Levite all need interpreting by the actors. They would need to speak as well. The Samaritan could speak to the wounded man and to the innkeeper. Other stories could demonstrate various things that might be interpretively added to make a story good drama rather than just role-playing.

143

Old Testament stories are rich in dialog and scenes as well as the stories of Jesus as examples for dramatizing. The point is still the same—the story is brought to life by the dialog and characters' actions. It is often a good practice to tell the verbatim Bible story either before as a way of familiarizing listeners with the story, or afterward to leave them with the authentic account from God's Word now that they are familiar with the story from seeing the visualized drama.

## Sung Story

The sung story may be a chronologically arranged ballad in which the song progresses through the storyline. Or the sung story may be versified as it is broken up into episodes, themes or scenes and sung along with a chorus that is a summary or comment on all the verses. Among many oral peoples it is not uncommon for the chorus to be a kind of refrain in which the listeners can join. In an earlier example I mentioned a song format among the Kui tribal people called *das katha*. The singers sing a verse and then click two sticks together rhythmically as they dance and sing the refrain. When the refrain is ended, the singers move on to the next verse. I witnessed the story of Jonah presented as *das katha* that lasted several hours. The large crowd enjoyed the performance immensely.

While in Pakistan, at the conclusion of a training session with Punjabis, an old man asked permission to sing the story of Jonah. It lasted about 15 minutes and appeared to be more of a ballad style song. The man sang without any accompaniment.

I was in New Mexico meeting with some Navajo friends. A Navajo pastor who has a radio program told of singing a song about the return of Jesus. There was a very good response from radio listeners saying they had never heard that story before. After telling about his experience the pastor then sang the song. He realized that scripture story songs in his Navajo language would speak in a way that could attract many of his people to the Gospel.

So the Bible story is either crafted into component parts for verses that emphasize some action or words, or is molded into a flowing story that is narrated musically as a ballad. Words may be rearranged or added, and altered to accommodate the rhythm or to produce a poetic rhyming. It is common for phrases to be repeated in the course of the song.

### Recast Story

Some of the Gospel stories like *The Prodigal Son* or *Two Men Who Went to the Temple to Pray* can be recast easily into a different time and place. The object is to keep the basic storyline, but to change location of the story, the names of the characters, or any other thing that might be a factor in helping listeners accept and relate to the story. One simple form of recasting a story leaves out details about location or names of characters so that the listeners, in hearing the story, recast it in their own mind as they interpret the story to fit their own experiences and knowledge. This was done in the story of the *Exalted Sacrifice* used in a booklet in Indonesia where the name of Isaac was not mentioned, only calling him Abraham's son. I suppose this was done deliberately to keep the reader's focus on the Substitute Sacrifice and not to be put off by mentioning Isaac by name. I understand why this was done, but have mixed feelings about the deception when using a near verbatim story.

One year a studio in Saigon produced a recasting of *The Prodigal Son* story. In the movie the story took place in modern day Saigon and the flashback that was the story began when an elderly grandfather began telling his grandson a story about someone he knew who demanded his inheritance and then ran away and wasted the inheritance. Finally when the inheritance was gone and the person was hungry he returned home to beg his father's forgiveness and ask to be a servant in his father's house. The flashback ended as the grandfather and son began their walk home. The grandson said that it was a good story but it probably did not happen—it was just a story. The grandfather stopped and looked at his grandson and said, "But it is a true story that really happened." The grandson replied, "How do you know it is a true story?" Then the grandfather with tears in his eyes said, I know it is a true story because I know the person. That person is your father." And so the movie ended.

It is always a bit shocking to hear a story well known to us redeveloped in a different way. But it can be a very powerful way of calling attention to a Bible story by making the basic storyline more relational for listeners who may have doubts about the Bible stories being ancient stories or stories that happened in another land among different people and so don't relate to people today. The idea is not to rewrite the Bible story, but to capture the attention of listeners who may not only be resistant to "Christian" teaching but also suspicious and possibly hostile to it. So the recast story provides a nonthreatening story that a listener can hear and possibly find their place in the story. In situations like this a recast Bible story should always be followed by the source Bible story to bring a spiritual dimension to the relational aspect of the recast story. One way to use a story like this with literates is to tell it and then have the listeners break up into buzz groups to talk about the story. When the groups reassemble the source story is told and discussed to see how the listeners related to the recast story and then what the source Bible story said to them.

Obviously, a storyer would want to be careful about using a recast Bible story where it might be confused with the original Bible story. So a recast story would not be good for those listeners where an oral Bible was being developed. But among literate post moderns who can read the original source story this is a possibility. Recast

Bible stories may find greater use in story sermons, again among literate listeners or, if carefully set-apart, with some selected oral learners.

For an example of a possible recasting of the well-known *Prodigal Son* Bible story visit the *Sermonstorying* website.[49] Under the heading *Articles* go to "Using Recast Bible Stories" to find *The Prodigal Daughter*. The storyline is the same, the gender is changed, and the setting is in a small town.

Here are some other stories that can be recast. The story of Joseph that considers both the issues of jealousy and forgiveness. Coveteousness and disobedience are themes in the story of Achan and the Destruction of Ai. In some cultures a recast story of Ruth could be very powerful showing a good outcome to a tragic life. Several of the teaching parables of Jesus lend themselves to recasting. *The Parable of The Wise and Foolish Builders* in Matthew 7, the *Parables of the Hidden Treasure* and *The Pearl* in Matthew 13, the *Parable of the Unmerciful Servant* in Matthew 18, the *Parable of the Two Sons* in Matthew 21, the *Parable of The Ten Lepers* in Luke 17 illustrates one who was thankful and nine who failed to failed to thank their benefactor, the *Parable of the Great Banquet* where the guests declined their invitations in Luke 14, and the *Parable of the Shrewd Manager* are just a few of the many possibilities for recasting Bible stories.

While the greater part of this book has related to oral communicators and to a lesser extent to those hostile to traditional Christian teaching, there are also many post modern and other young people who may initially respond to a recast story that somehow puts the story and its teaching into their world. My personal practice is always to follow the recast story and any discussion with the source Bible story. If using such stories poses a problem for you, then I suggest that you not use them.

# Chapter 13

## Oralizing Considerations
## For An Oral Bible

Considerations for an Oral Bible are a bit different. The term Oral Bible was an expression I begun using back in the early 1990s among the rural Koch and Tripura people in Bangladesh and tribal Kui in Orissa, India. It was during the time that I was intensively training rural pastors and evangelists to know the Bible in a form they could remember and recall in their ministry. It struck me one day that since many of these workers could not read the Bible and, in several places had no translated Bible in their spoken language, that all the Bible they possessed was what they had heard and remembered.

Perhaps I should have used a term like "Memory Scriptures" or some other expression that would not cause reaction like the term "Oral Bible." I have been reminded many times that the Bible is a "book." I shared my thinking about the Oral Bible observation with a colleague I was co-teaching with in other countries and the term became part of our shared vocabulary. He went on to develop a guide for giving people an Oral Bible.[50] While the guide is helpful in all its considerations, it went beyond what I was observing happening at the time.

Sometime later a strategy was developing to make the basic evangelism and church planting Scriptures available to those lacking Scripture in their spoken language. This was then broadened to include a deliberate strategy to provide in effect additional oral Scripture for those living in oral cultures and lacking adequate literacy to read available Bibles, or lacking translated Scripture in their spoken language. This was to be a stopgap effort to make Scripture widely quickly available to oral cultures. And it was to be the initiation of effort in the long term to provide access to key oral or written Scripture and eventually a whole translated Bible. There was never an

149

intention to replace properly translated written Scripture, nor to deny any persons living in oral cultures access to the whole counsel of God. The term Oral Bible has spread and now seems to be widely accepted among those in the Great Commission Christian world. While the Bible translation process has sped up considerably in recent years, the need will remain for oral Scriptures for many years to come. So where to start and how does Oralizing Bible Stories for Telling fit in?

I use the term "tension" a good bit in describing the various considerations and limits faced by the Bible storyer. In the case of the Oral Bible the tension exists between access to the whole verbatim counsel of God and the practical limits of oral memory and typical use of Scripture in daily living and worship.

An oral communicator is limited to knowledge coming from others in oral form or from his/her own memory. While memory for oral communicators may be quite good, it is not infinite, and usually has a practical limit to what is needed in their daily life, what works or helps them to understand the world they live in, and their heritage stories. Information that is seldom used is often lost as new practical information replaces it. Oral learning for most comes through repeated hearing of information in a form that is memorable. Here another tension exists. For the literate teacher it is often a challenge to format and simplify the message for oral learners, and then have patience to repeat it as often as needed until learning takes place. Participation by oral learners like retelling of stories or group memorizing of passages helps the learning process.

Any teaching that is done must clearly delineate what is Bible and what is not Bible. This is why deeply paraphrased Bible stories are to be avoided, as anything contained in the context of the story is Bible to the listener who can't read the story and decide for himself/herself.

Further, stories provide the "baskets" mentioned earlier as containers for biblical truth. So stories provide the bulk of the teaching, as stories are a coherent form of packaging information. Relevant memory verses also seem to work well. And to a limited extent longer memorized passages may be retained by young people who are avid learners, and older members of a community that have the task of remembering and recalling significant group history and other information deemed important by the group.

Oral learners enjoy learning in community as a group. This is fortunate as it provides the venue for story repetition as listeners participate. And it provides a corrective in the form of the "group story" in that, as the group learns the stories, if any member of the group changes a story, the group is there to correct the story. I have seen this as it happened in Bible Storying teaching sessions and in a Bible Storying camp where the campers were energetically correcting one another as they participated in the Bible story retelling.

Bible stories like any other items we remember can fade over time if not periodically refreshed or exercised. Hearing the stories again helps to refresh the stories. Telling the stories to others exercises the stories to keep them fresh in the memory.

Oralizing Bible stories for an Oral Bible then typically begins with providing an representative Bible that contains a panoramic overview of the Bible that contains essential evangelistic, church planting and discipling stories, memory verses and key narrative passages. During the time that I was engaged in teaching the Bible stories among Asian peoples I observed that listeners had an optimum learning speed. This was illustrated in a project in southern Sudan among nonliterate seminary students that five new stories a week were too many but three new stories could be handled by the students. And I observed that without frequent review of earlier stories,

151

there was fading if the Bible Storying teaching was too long from beginning to closure. In those days it seemed that a two-year cycle was about optimum and practical as it provided opportunity for a new story each week and adequate review of earlier stories.

The Bible stories were chosen based primarily on the truths needed for each objective—evangelism, church planting, discipling or leader training. Attention was given to spiritual worldview and certain cultural issues that affected story choice and story formatting for telling.

During the time I was conducting five-day Bible Storying training sessions for leaders I had pre-selected the stories to be used from my working knowledge of the local spiritual worldview, culture, and key stories needed for evangelizing, planting a church, discipling and training emerging church leaders. This resulted in between 65 to 80 stories that I covered as I prepared widely not knowing exactly which stories would be most relevant. To select a short list of stories I associated each Bible story with a teaching picture. Then I placed all the pictures on a table and let the group work around the table to select the pictures that represented the stories they felt best spoke to their people. This most often resulted in 35 to 40 pictures they intuitively selected. I quickly reviewed these stories in a chronological order though I later observed that when the trainees were telling the Bible stories among their own people that they did not always observe the chronological sequence, but instead through some logic of their own selected stories in a sequence that made sense to them. At first this was distressing to me as I saw the needed progression from chronological story to story. But then I relaxed as I thought about their own form of CBS—"Chaotic Bible Storying!" What was rewarding is that the trainees were indeed telling the stories and their people were listening.

During these early days of teaching Bible stories I did not use any written Bible Storying notes or written stories. As I worked with my interpreters I soon settled into a pattern of oralizing shaped by my experience with my interpreter and response of the trainees. Many of the considerations that I have shared in the previous chapters come from these experiences over that thirteen-year period from 1988 until 2001 when I returned to the U.S. to retire.

I realized that during this time I was providing for many of these nonliterate leaders an Oral Bible that increased each time I met with them and added new stories. I would have loved to provide more teaching in each place but this would have denied others the opportunity to learn. During this time I learned quite fluently around one hundred stories from which I could pick and choose while teaching, or use in radio listener follow-up ministry, or while preaching in their churches.

Eventually some of these people gained access to a translated Bible in their spoken language. Some were able to "read" their Bibles after they first learned the stories orally. Others still need to hear someone tell them the Bible stories so they can learn them. In recent years the Training for Trainers methodology has been wedded to the use of Bible stories and is called *Storying Training for Trainers* (ST4T).[51] In Karnataka State, South India, this novel approach of training using Bible stories is equipping pastors, many with little or no literacy, to teach key Bible stories to their church members who are then encouraged to go out into their neighborhoods and communities to tell the stories and plant new house churches.

In one report I heard while in India, children were reading Bible stories to an older nonliterate pastor until he was able to learn the stories. Then he preached/told the stories to his congregation and repeated the stories several times so the congregation could learn them and even had the congregation to repeat the stories back to him. Then he would send the congregation out to tell the stories. I suspect that any oralizing done to the stories was done purely intuitively.

So in this chapter I do not propose any strict rules regarding oralizing Bible stories for Oral Bibles. My preference would be the simplest crafting needed while staying as close to verbatim as possible. Many of the shorter Bible stories and especially the parables and miracle stories of Jesus are good to go as is and can be used virtually verbatim. I did make the pronoun replacement and the character dialog changes that I mentioned earlier.

Others are using digital devices like *MegaVoice*[52] players or Faith Comes By Hearing's *Proclaimer*[53] to provide unlimited repetition of selected Bible stories or verse-by-verse read Scripture to teach oral learners. These devices have the ability to continually refresh the Bible stories for listeners. One lady in Thailand many years ago said about the stories coming from an audiocassette player: "The machine always tells the story the same way every time!"

While the digital players can endlessly repeat the stories, I believe that the live telling of the Bible stories will for the future remain the most reproducible way to teach God's Word to an oral learner world. This means that someone who can read the stories must learn them and then reliably retell and teach the stories to oral learners. Teachers and trainers should watch what the oral learners do with the Bible stories and learn from them how best to oralize the Bible stories for understanding and reproducibility.

# Chapter 14

## Oralizing Bible Stories
## For Preaching

One of the ongoing concerns where rapid church planting is taking place is how to equip and empower oral leaders who will be serving as pastor for the newly planted churches. In many places literacy is low and orality is the *de facto* communication mode.

In my own early years of teaching Bible stories for leaders, most of those who came for training were either nonliterate or ranged from barely literate to semiliterate and had little formal education. Among these were men called to preach and pastor who had few skills for Bible study, some had no Bible yet in their spoken language, and those who were literate had no study resources beyond a Bible with no helps. Many of the men asked questions about how to preach certain Bible stories. Or they wanted to talk about the things in the stories so they could understand the stories well enough to develop messages. I tried to reserve some time for the men to ask questions so that I could point them back to what the Bible had to say. Those who had Bibles and could read wanted to look at the stories and ask background questions and questions about interpretation of the difficult passages. When asked these questions I always tried to use the Bible to interpret the Bible by taking the pastors to other scripture passages that helped to answer their questions.

Much of this was initiated by the panorama of the Bible stories that helped the men to see the connectedness of the stories, and the other was hearing the stories told in an understandable way that opened up the stories to their curiosity and interest. Several of my interpreters were very helpful during these times. Often the literate men asked for notes or helps. Where notes in the local language were needed, interpreters were gracious to help me provide these. On occasion I would prepare some simple helps that included parallel scripture passages rather than to provide my own interpretation. I wanted them to look to the Bible first for understanding. If I could have changed anything during those days, it would have been to have a mobile Bible school so that I could visit in their area to teach rather than having them to leave their families to come to a center or camp for teaching. They knew that I had a Bible (Thompson Chain Reference) that had many helps in it. After some time teaching the Bible stories, I learned most of the questions the men would ask so that I did not need to refer to my Bible helps for answers.

Because the men were hearing the stories told in a way they could easily understand, it was opening the Bible up for them to want to know more. Oh, we had some of the usual questions like why did God accept Abel's offering and reject Cain's? or the old question of where did Cain get his wife? One literate older pastor even wanted to know more about King Solomon's many concubines. I didn't want to waste time on stories like this with the training group, but did enjoy talking with the pastor over a cup of tea in his home.

What was exciting to most pastors were the prophecies and promises in the Old Testament and seeing them fulfilled in later Old Testament stories and especially in the Gospel stories of Jesus. Also the men were attracted to story clusters where a group of stories had a common theme. I had demonstrated using these when asked to preach. I usually asked literate pastors in the larger churches if they minded if I preached a story sermon rather than a typical expositional (Western style) sermon. If they did mind I would decline preaching in their churches. If they begrudgingly gave me permission I used oralized stories but then added exposition following each story. I had wanted to model for pastors—all pastors, not just the nonliterate pastors, that it was okay to preach story sermons. Their congregations responded well to the oralized stories and several commented about the stories when I visited their churches later. Some of the untrained pastors asked for copies of the story sermons to use in their churches.

The nonliterate pastors did not have all these story guidelines to follow for oralizing their stories in preaching. They did intuitively what I have been suggesting as guidelines. Once they heard the stories the pastors adapted the stories for their people, still as stories.

So for those pastors lacking Bibles in their spoken language, hearing the oralized stories became their resource for preaching. For literate pastors lacking any study resources in either English or their spoken language the oralized stories and our discussions about the stories in training sessions were their resource for sermons.

For the nonliterate pastors the Oral Bible concept is most important because it gives them access to common stories they can use for evangelism and strengthening their members. So all of this is interrelated.

It is important for resident missionaries and for visiting short-term mission teams to continue modeling for both the pastors and their congregations story sermons using Bible stories oralized for easy comprehension and recall. This need will continue for the future as new churches are planted and more are called to pastor the churches. Most of these new pastors will be one or more of the following: nonliterate, marginally literate so that study of the Bible is difficult, lack a Bible in their spoken language, have little or no theological training, or have hermeneutical study resources. So learning the stories is a first step for many new pastors so they can preach appropriate sermons for their congregations.

During the time I was still working in South Asia two of the missionaries serving as agriculturists among the

Kui people began training pastors to use Bible stories. I had been traveling through the tribal area teaching three to five day conferences for pastors in churches. John Langston at an agricultural training center invited a large number of Kui pastors to come for several weeks of agricultural training to learn how to provide food for their families during the hot dry season. During this time his staff conducted several hours of Bible story teaching and practicum each day.

After John left another missionary from the Philippines who had training and experience in using Bible Storying came as the new agriculturist. Not only did he encourage the staff to continue the Bible story training, but Calvin Fox had a real burden for the pastors and equipping them to preach appropriate oral learner sermons for their people using Bible stories.

Another missionary with a different organization has been conducting Bible story training for pastors in India for over ten years. The pastors for the most part are literate and many have some theological education. But their congregations have low literacy and most are oral learners. The pastors have been reporting amazing response of their people to the stories with many families coming to faith in Christ, and perhaps the most amazing of all, is that the people believe the Bible stories and expect miracles just like happened in the stories—and they do!

I'll end this chapter with a quote from this missionary in one of his reports.

> *Literate believers are usually taught God's promises as propositional statements of what God will do for us in response to our faith. But because oral communicators have not learned to think in literate patterns, such promises have little meaning for them. In contrast, a Bible story is a technicolor promise full of sound and action, populated by living people who faced danger and were rescued by God.*[54]

158

# Chapter 15

## Limitations for
## Training Oral Leaders

I nearly forgot this chapter and was reminded only a short time ago by a colleague I have been exchanging notes with. He was expressing concern about making formatting changes in preparing Bible stories for telling that a nonliterate leader or one who was literate but untrained would not be able to replicate. Specifically he was asking about enhanced (harmonized) stories that are drawn from several parallel accounts. And he was right. I have been involved with Bible Storying so long that I tend to do things intuitively as a communicator. In the early days I had only two model story sets that were paraphrased stories and several lists of Bible stories, but no methodology guidelines, so all had to be learned.

This is doubly embarrassing because of what I earlier wrote in the *People-Powered Media* paper and what Chris Ammons wrote in his *Third Generation Thinking* paper. Both should be a reminder not to do anything that those being trained cannot do. And I confess that I observed this in my training days. However, I also spent much time telling the Bible stories in public proclamation rallies related to radio listener follow-up and from invitations by local pastors to use the Bible Storying occasion as an evangelism rally they could later follow up.

I had intuitively begun doing story crafting as I prepared the Bible stories for strategies in villages, training oral leaders, and the public rallies. Perhaps the problem began when others asked me what I was doing and how I did it. I should have made a clearer distinction between the evangelism proclamation and leader training. Also I need to defend what I have done and taught as I also engaged literate peoples who could read the Bible and so were able to read the source stories and then hear how I combined them into more detailed stories. Even today as Bible Storying is considered more and more as a very productive small group discipling method, the need for some of the oralizing format changes are still valid for literates, even if not valid for all nonliterates.

So what can be used with nonliterates without causing problems later on? Part of the question hinges on what is "Oral Bible?" How much adapting can be done and we still call the stories as "Oral Bible?" For those today who are working to provide an Oral Bible for nonliterates and those lacking a Bible, what formatting is desirable? For those working with literates, whether on a mission field or in the U.S., are these formatting options still viable?

As a communicator I had an objective leading to desired result which was to see listeners come to faith in Jesus as Savior, to plant a viable New Testament church, to begin the discipling process, and to empower emerging church leaders. I was less concerned about form (format) than I was regarding function—results.

The first Bible Storying lesson models I was acquainted with used deeply paraphrased stories sometimes with a bit of exposition or commentary added into the stories. Later as I realized the need to go back to the Bible and develop the stories I needed in my outreach strategies I went to the verbatim stories. Pretty soon I realized the need to clarify the stories from the standpoint of my telling them through an interpreter. And for the benefit of the listeners to be able easily to follow the stories, to experience them relationally, and to remember the stories that some adaptation was often needed. I saw the changes these early listeners made to the stories when they retold them. I responded by first trying to correct the listeners by repeating the stories many times and later by taking into account some of the changes they were intuitively making as they retold the stories. As I mentioned earlier in the chapter on stories being altered by listeners, I began to anticipate some of these changes so the listeners would have less processing to do when they retold the stories. So I began to pre-adapt some stories to be sure the right things were kept as part of the stories and not dropped or confused in the retelling.

Still later as the concept of using Bible Storying spread to the literate world, I saw the opportunity of creatively formatting selected stories for greater relevance, for stronger emphasis, and in some cases for a clearer understanding of background or consequences of what happened in the stories. My intention was not to edit or change the Bible, but to communicate what was in it more effectively in the process of taking the stories from the printed page to be told orally as interesting and effective stories. This was not to displace the work of the Holy Spirit in His ministry to convince of sin, but to "break the bread of righteousness" to distribute it to listeners so they could hear it to their fill.

## Considerations for Training Oral Leaders

The ideal Bible story in all situations is the verbatim story, altering no wording or way the story is expressed. This assumes that Bible translators have done a thorough study of culture and language for accurate expression of key terms. We realize that language is dynamic and that variations do exist in dialects, in local culture, and among those of different spiritual backgrounds. For some of these like Muslims that already have bias against the Bible the verbatim may be best received and the safest to use.

For others like some of the deep rural and tribal peoples I encountered, their everyday vocabularies were limited, making it difficult to understand some stories and discourse passages even though properly translated. Other considerations like pronoun substitution if used in local translations might need consideration. The bottom line for testing verbatim stories is to tell them verbatim to listeners and see what listeners do as they attempt to retell the same stories. What do they keep, what do they omit, what do they alter as they retell each story?

The limited verbatim story with minimal editing to remove some of the confusing details without changing the other wording might be a good compromise. Limited verbatim editing moves the story a bit closer to the way that some of the less able listeners might attempt to retell the story. Again, try this with stories that listeners struggle with and see if it helps them to accurately retain the significant portions of the story in their retelling.

Basic crafting would be the next level in which numbers, especially large numbers, are expressed as concrete-relational similes, and other numbers, unless needed for the story to make sense, might also be expressed as similes or dropped out.

Character dialog could follow the guidelines suggested earlier in substituting proper names or nouns for pronouns (especially in the Gospel stories) and placing the speaker-to-listener reference before the dialog so it is clear who is speaking to whom.

In the case of longer stories (such as the Flood Story, the Joseph Story, the Plagues and Passover story(ies), or the Jonah Story) some condensing of the story by light paraphrasing could make the stories more manageable for listeners. This procedure doesn't compromise biblical accuracy.

Compiled stories like *Creation of the Spirit World* or a *Prophecies of the Messiah* story could be used if needed. Story clusters should not be a problem, but harmonized stories could be a problem. I would avoid recast stories unless used in preaching and not teaching. I would leave the matter of singing or dancing the stories up to local listeners if they desire to express the stories that way. Drama should be effective to illustrate the otherwise verbatim or near-verbatim stories.

# Chapter 16

## It's Your Decision

To Oralize Bible stories for telling or not? Does any hesitation about crafting or rewording Bible stories for telling remain? One way to settle the matter is to begin telling the Bible stories in whatever form the storyer is comfortable with and see what the listeners do with the stories in their retelling to others. A concern that I always had when telling the Bible stories in public places where many people gathered is that some of the listeners may hear the Bible stories only that one time. Will they be able to understand and grasp the implication for their lives? Will they be able to remember the stories and possibly take the stories home to other family members or neighbors? Many children have heard Bible stories and taken the stories home to their parents and siblings resulting in families coming to faith in Christ.

I have worked with at least three cultures where the Bible was in a high literary language that was proper for a holy book. In these cultures, the Bible was not in the type of language that people spoke in everyday life. The literary form may have been lovely to hear, but if the verbatim words and meaning of the stories are not clear, then what is gained? There are cultures that believe merit is gained by simply hearing the sounds of the words whether the meaning is understood or not. This may be entertaining, but such hearing does not lead to understanding about God and His relationship with mankind leading to a restored relationship through forgiveness and the salvation Jesus provided.

We are to treat God's Word with reverence and caution. But at the same time we see in the Bible itself that when earlier stories were told at later times, stories were summarized or told according to the existing need or situation. Jesus referred to several stories like Noah, Jonah, and the Bronze Serpent without retelling the story

163

verbatim. We don't know how much detail Jesus included in his two stories in the Nazareth synagogue when he mentioned Namaan the leper and his healing and the widow of Zarephath, both of whom were not Israelites.

In order to see church planting movements continue to gain momentum, the Bible needs to be inserted into a people's culture in an understandable form and turned loose. Telling Bible stories in person or through various recorded digital media may do this. Stories will need to be carefully selected and matched for each people group and then crafted into a "tellable" form that is understandable and memorable so that anyone who hears the stories might be able easily and accurately to pass them along to others.

An additional thought regards crafting Bible stories for singing. In many oral cultures people remember important stories by singing. This occasions some adapting of Bible stories for the singing format that may be a ballad style that recounts the whole story or verses that sing about characteristics and the work of God. We may not be able to develop the story songs ourselves, but local people can, if they hear the stories in a form that helps in the transition from told story to sung story.

Most of what I have shared in these chapters comes from my own personal experience. In the beginning I had nothing but the paraphrased story models from the Philippines to use. I confess that I did not in the beginning think clearly about the need for adapting the Bible stories for the various peoples I would encounter and have opportunity to teach. Soon I realized that the power was in the stories and not in the accompanying teaching. And I realized the effect of listeners' worldview on story choice and crafting or adapting for telling.

It was apparent that the original lengthy Chronological Bible Storying strategies were being joined by many new opportunities for different story sets, shorter story sets, and appropriately crafted stories to take maximum advantage of each occasion.

Yet the respect for the verbatim story was always present. Among storyers there was a tension on whatever crafting was done to adapt Bible stories for each new situation. Such feelings are easily understood.

I've been challenged a number of times about story crafting or oralizing as I now prefer to call it. But after many years among people who needed simplified stories they could understand and replicate, I am satisfied that oralizing that always keeps the verbatim Bible story in view is the best of both worlds. Until a time comes when God's Word can be put into everyday conversational language among the entire world's people, published in affordable formats, and the people acquire the needed literacy to read for themselves and understand what they are reading, then I suspect there will be the need for oralized Bible stories.

Earlier I had mentioned praying for wisdom and guidance in preparing the stories. This is essential. It is not our cleverness in adapting Bible stories that leads to blessing and understanding. We are in a partnership with the Holy Spirit. The Bible has in effect been translated and adapted for us to read with comprehension. For oral learners we continue the task of adapting the Bible stories for hearing with comprehension.

If there are questions and a reader wants to ask or exchange thoughts regarding the process of oralizing Bible stories for telling I would welcome the opportunity. I do not intend to debate whether oralizing or crafting Bible stories is good or not. I settled that issue personally a long time ago. I rejoice at seeing the many nonliterate leaders and their people come to a saving knowledge of Jesus through hearing the prepared stories.

The story sets that I have shared are only models that approximate how I told the stories as each situation and opportunity was a bit different in some way. I do not encourage new storyers simply to take any of my story sets and use them without careful review and adapting as needed. Preferably I would encourage storyers to look at my models and then go back to the people's Scriptures and develop the stories fresh from that and not from what I have crafted. You do not need to agree with my story oralizing. If I have only raised your awareness of shaping a written story for telling, then I have accomplished my objective. My versions of the stories are only models to demonstrate the oralizing process and possibilities.

In conclusion, The Bible writers have done a wonderful job of telling and recording the stories. Bible translators have done a wonderful work of putting the stories into good English or other languages and into an acceptable grammatical style that a holy book is worthy of possessing. But we don't always speak the way we write—we take shortcuts at times and usually avoid overly long, detailed or complex statements.

If we are oral learners, we have a talking style that reflects a simpler and clearer way of organizing our thoughts and expressing them in ways commonly acceptable, understandable, and enjoyable by our listeners. So when we tell the Bible stories we attempt to oralize them for good telling while respecting the sanctity of the Word and being mindful of spiritual needs and abilities of our listeners to hear the stories accurately and even be able to repeat them.

Fortunately, many of the Bible stories are either good to go *as is*, or need only minor crafting to make them understandable and memorable. Much of what I have suggested about story crafting or oralizing the new Bible storyer will in time learn to do intuitively as he/she prepares the stories for their people and tells the stories.

How the listeners retell the stories will suggest crafting needs to make them good oral versions. If a story is too difficult to remember and retell correctly by listeners, then it may also be too difficult to understand clearly or confusing to listeners. If the story is difficult for the storyer to remember and tell correctly then some crafting may be needed to make the story more memorable and easier to tell.

We use the expression "sola scriptura" to say that only the Scriptures are the authority. Our task and role is to help especially nonliterates to have access to those Scriptures. Then we can say, "To God be the glory!"

# Definitions

*Allegory*—An allegory is a symbolic representation that parallels or illustrates a deeper meaning that is not readily apparent in the wording. Some believe that all or most Bible stories are in fact allegorical implying deeper meaning than is at first apparent. Such persons may believe they possess the key to interpret or unlock the allegory. Others believe that there may be allegory but that Scripture is plain and understandable and that Scripture interprets Scripture and the Holy Spirit gives understanding.

*Concrete Relational Thinking*—This term relates to the practice of using concrete references like similes rather than abstractions, especially in regard to quantities like numbers or dimensions. For instance "3,000" may be meaningless to oral listeners but by comparing it to trees in the forest or stars in the sky suggests a great quantity.

*Crafting*—This term replaced the original term "editing" which seemed to imply re-arranging or over-correcting the Bible stories. Part of the concept is that of shaping the stories or simply polishing or touching up the written stories to make them good oral accounts for maximum comprehension when telling.

*Oralizing*—This term is a more current use that includes the concept of crafting stories for telling, but with a reminder that the reason for crafting the stories is to make them good oral accounts for telling. For me it will in time replace the former term "crafting."

*Negative Restructuring*—This term describes the intuitive process that is the reinterpretation of stories to bring them into line with a listener's culture or spiritual worldview. It in effect means interpreting or changing the meaning away from the original in support of other existing beliefs. Use of story clusters or story series helps to discourage this happening as the other stories help to lock in intended meaning.

*Recast Stories*—These are stories that are reset into another time, location, or with different characters, though the basic storyline remains the same. There are several reasons for doing this. One is to avoid or skirt some hostility issues while covering the basic truths. Another is to make the story more relational to listeners—"like them," easier to identify with. And a third is simply to gain listener's attention by using a story that is not necessarily identifiable as biblical.

*Stereotyping*—This practice labels characters usually by combining a descriptive term with a name, especially to help distinguish a person by some characteristic. Ex: Prophet Elijah, Ehud the left-handed. And help to distinguish among characters with similar names like Elijah and Elisha.

*Story Scripting*—Paul Koehler uses this term in place of story crafting. He defines it as phrasing Bible stories so they will be memorable to the listener like the original was to the original listener, while bringing the story into the listener's own context as much as possible.[55]

*Story Smithing*—Tom Steffen uses this the term in place of story crafting. The idea is that of shaping a story to full usefulness so the story becomes context-specific, yet remains accurate biblically.[56]

*Threads*—These are verbal connections that may be repeated words or phrases that tie a story together by showing connectedness or that stress some characteristic or theme. Three times it is said that Noah obeyed all that God commanded him to do. The same character found in several successive stories is a thread linking the stories, for instance the stories of Abraham, Isaac, Jacob, or Joseph. Repeated promises are also threads linking stories.

# Resources

Barry McWilliams, *Discerning the Story Structures In the Narrative Literature of the Bible.*

A helpful study for preparation of stories for telling by understanding the story structure. His *Steps in Story Analysis* is good.
*http://www.eldrbarry.net/mous/bibl/narr.htm*

Barry McWilliams, *Effective Storytelling: A Manual for Beginners.*

Another good read on the spectrum of storytelling.
*http://www.eldrbarry.net/roos/eest.htm.*

*Children's Bible Stories in Easy English.*

These 54 stories for children were originally downloaded from an Internet site that is no longer posted. If interested contact *jot2@iname.com*.

Jesse Lyman Hurlbut, *Bedtime Bible Story Book*, Barbour Books, Barbour and Company, Inc., 1989 paper.

Popular because it contains 365 chronologically arranged Bible stories prepared for reading to children. The stories are crafted probably for older children and in several instances vary slightly from Bible details.

Johnston M. Cheney & Stanley Ellisen, *The Greatest Story*, Multnomah Books, Questar Publishers, 1994.

A unique harmonizing of the four Gospels into one single set of Gospel stories by combining details from all four Gospels around one selected as the key account. Especially helpful for the *Birth Narrative* and the *Passion Story* accounts.

*Garden of Praise* Children's Bible Lessons—Includes 87 Bible stories worded for children along with activities for teaching the stories.

*http://www.gardenofpraise.com/bibleles.htm#new.*

171

Global Recordings Network, *Look, Listen & Live* series.

The LLL scripts provide one-paragraph stories or multi-paragraph stories that some have found helpful as condensed paraphrases. Scripts developed to accompany picture booklets and flipcharts. *http://globalrecordings.net/topic/audiovisuals.*

*God's Story for Children* (Children's Chapel).

Each of these online free resource stories contains a retelling of the Bible story, questions to think about (great for introducing the story), a special lesson to remember, a Scripture memory verse, a prayer, where the story can be found in the Bible, and usually activities, crafts, and songs to go along with the story. *http://childrenschapel.org/bibstory2.html.*

Kurt Jarvis, (*www.CBS4Kids.org*) International Network for Children's Ministry.

Kurt and his wife Judy have 40 years of experience working children here in the U.S. and internationally. When Kurt learned about CBS he adapted the chronological Bible Storying to age-graded curriculum for children. His manual *Bible Storying and the Bible Story Quilt for Kids* is unique. Also *kurtnjudy@yahoo.com.*

Paul F. Koehler, *Telling God's Stories With Power: Biblical Storytelling in Oral Cultures*, William Carey Library, 2010 paper.

Koehler's experiences serving with a large indigenous church-planting organization in South Asia led to a search for a more effective way of communicating the Bible and training storytellers from a wide range of people groups. A complete and practical introduction to biblical storytelling in cross-cultural contexts.

Richard L. Pratt, *He Gave Us Stories* (The Bible Student's Guide to Interpreting Old Testament Narratives), Presbyterian & Reformed Publishing Co., 1993 paper.

A helpful text for analyzing Old Testament narrative principles when crafting Old Testament stories.

Ted Miller (adapted by) *The Story from The Book* (*From Adam to Armageddon*), Tyndale House, 1987 paper.

172

A chronological narrative account of the Bible story told by episodes without book, chapter or verse references. The stories are condensed from the Living Bible account and are harmonized by combining the kingdom and prophet stories, the four Gospel accounts, and Acts and the Epistles into unified stories. It has value in suggesting how to tell some of the stories that have been harmonized and interwoven.

Tom A. Steffen, *Reconnecting God's Story to Ministry: Crosscultural Storytelling at Home and Abroad*, Center for Organizational and Ministry Development, La Habra, 1996.

A basic text on selecting, preparing and using Bible stories in ministry. Steffen was a New Tribes missionary who began using the chronological Bible teaching lessons and later realized that his people learned and responded better to telling the Bible stories. Steffen now teaches Intercultural Studies at Biola University. His book uses slightly different vocabulary but the same basic concepts.

Tom A. Steffen, *Passing the Baton: Church Planting That Empowers*, Center for Organizational and Ministry Development, la Habra, 1993, 1997.

Steffen explores exit strategy needed by the missionary. The book has a review of Steffen's experience as a pioneer with Chronological Bible Teaching and discovery of the power of stories with his tribal people group.

# List of Stories

# References

[1] Dell G. Schultze and Rachel Sue Schultze, *God and Man*, New Tribes Mission, Manila,1984.

[2] Caloy Gabuco, *"Telling the Story..."*, New Tribes Mission and International Mission Board, Manila, 1987.

[3] J.O.Terry, "People-Powered Media," unpublished paper, December 1991.

[4] Chris Ammons, "Third Generation Thinking," unpublished paper.

[5] J.O.Terry, "Crafting Bible Stories for Telling," *Basic Bible Storying*, Church Starting Network, Fort Worth, 2006.

[6] LaNette Thompson, "Diaradugu Diary," International Mission Board, SBC,unpublished report.

[7] Steve Baker, "Storying in Malawi, Event in Process", unpublished case study, 1992.

[8] Tom A. Steffen, *Reconnecting God's Story to Ministry: Crosscultural Storytelling at Home and Abroad*, Center for Organizational and Ministry Development, La Habra, CA, 1996.

[9] Paul F. Koehler, *Telling God's Stories With Power: Biblical Storytelling in Oral Cultures*, William Carey Library, 2010. pp 110-117.

[10] Grant Lovejoy in an email dated 3/23/09.

[11] Kirin Narayan, *Storytellers, Saints, and Scoundrels*, University of Pennsylvania Press, 1989. pp. 114-115.

[12] J.O.Terry, *God and Woman*, International Mission Board, SBC, 1998.

[13] J.O.Terry, *Grief Stories from the Bible*, Church Starting Network, 2009.

[14] Read the whole account at: http://www.sacred-texts.com/nam/zuni/zft/zft33.htm.

[15] Jacob A. Loewen, "Bible Stories: Message and Matrix", *Culture and Human Values: Christian Intervention in Anthropological Perspective* (California: William Carey Library, 1975).

[16] Eugene A. Nida, Language Symbols and Meaning, Message and Mission: The Communication of the Christian Faith, rev. ed, Carey 1960/1990, 102.

[17] LaNette Thompson, *Diaradugu Diary*, unpublished paper of account of storying among Jula men and women of Burkina Faso.

[18] J.O.Terry, op cit.

[19] J.O.Terry, *Heaven Is For Women*, International Mission Board, May 2000.

[20] Johnston M. Cheney & Stanley Ellisen, *The Greatest Story*, Multnomah Books, Questar Publishers, Inc., 1994.

[21] Adapted by Ted Miller, *The Story: From the Book* (Adam to Armageddon), Tyndale House Publishers, Inc., 1986. (paper)

[22] Jesse Lyman Hurlbut, *365 Short Stories from the Bible*, Barbour Books, 1989.

[23] Ted Miller, op. cit.

[24] Dell and Sue Schultze, *God and Man*, New Tribes Mission, republished by Church Strengthening Ministry, Manila, Philippines.

[25] *Chronological Bible Storytelling—54 Bible Stories*, Church Strengthening Ministry, Manila, Philippines.

[26] Martin Goldsmith, as quoted in *Touching the Soul of Islam* by Bill A. Musk, MARC, 1995

[27] Jack Dean Kingsbury, *Matthew as Story* 2nd ed., rev. and enlarged, Fortress Press, 1988. p.10.

[28] Thomas E. Boomershine, *Story Journey: An Invitation to the Gospel as Storytelling*, Abingdon Press, 1988, p. 181. (Or go online to http://www.tomboomershine.org/pages/writings.html).

[29] J.O.Terry, *The Suffering Servant*, International Mission Board, September 2000.

[30] M. Kurt Jarvis, *Bible Storying and the Bible Story Quilt for Kids*, www.CBS4Kids.org, kurtnjudy@yahoo.com.

[31] Carla Clements, *Visual Story Bible Quilt*, www.BibleQuilt.org.

[32] *Look, Listen & Live*, Global Recordings Network, http://globalrecordings.net/topic/looklistenlive.

[33] Jesse Lyman Hurlbut, *Bedtime Bible Story Book*, Barbour & Company, 1989 paper.

[34] http://www.gardenofpraise.com/bible.es.htm#new.

[35] J.O.Terry, "The God Who Sees and Hears," *God and Woman*.

[36] J.O.Terry, "A Bride for Isaac," *God and Woman*.

[37] J.O.Terry, "The Sinful Woman Who Anointed Jesus," *God and Woman*.

38 J.O.Terry, "Jesus Restores a Widow's Only Son to Life," *God and Woman.*

39 J.O.Terry, "A Young Woman's Only Hope," *Grief Stories From the Bible,* Church Starting Network, Fort Worth.

40 J.O.Terry, "Change of Heart at the Bottom of the Sea," *Water Stories From the Bible,* Church Strengthening Network, Fort Worth.

41 J.O.Terry, "Jesus Thirsted so that We Might Freely Drink," *Water Stories From the Bible,* Church Strengthening Network, Fort Worth.

42 J.O.Terry, "Hope for a Paralyzed Man," *Hope Stories From the Bible,* Church Starting Network, Fort Worth.

43 Johnston M. Cheney & Stanley Ellisen, *The Greatest Story,* Mltnomah Books (Questar Publishers), 1969. Originally published as *The Life of Christ in Stereo,* Western Conservative Baptist Seminary, 1964.

44 J.O.Terry, "Food for the Hungry Multitude," *Food Stories from the Bible,* Church Starting Network, Fort Worth.

45 J.O.Terry, "Saul's Disobedience and Rejection as King," *Crafting Bible Stories for Telling,* unpublished training manual.

46 J.O.Terry, "God Judges David's Sin."

47 J.O.Terry, "God Created the Spirit World," *God and Woman.*

48 J.O.Terry, "The Promised One." *God and Woman.*

49 www.sermonstorying.110mb.com

50 James B. Slack, "Giving The Target People an Oral Bible," unpublished paper, November 1994.

51 Stephen Stringer, Gen. Editor, *Storying Training for Trainers,* http://www.st4t.org/.

52 MegaVoice, http://www.megavoice.com/.

53 Faith Comes by Hearing, *The Proclaimer,* http://www.faithcomesbyhearing.com/proclaimer.

54 Paul Mark, *Stories from Storytellers,* July 3, 2010.

55 Paul F. Koehler. (see Endnote 9)

56 Tom A. Steffen. (see Endnote 8, pp. 34-38, 133)